ONCE WE WERE SISTERS

ALSO BY SHEILA KOHLER

ONCE
WE
WERE
SISTERS

SHEILA KOHLER

CANONGATE

Published in Great Britain in 2017 by Canongate Books Ltd,
14 High Street, Edinburgh EH1 1TE

www.canongate.co.uk

1

First published in the United States by Penguin Books, an imprint of
Penguin Random House LLC, 375 Hudson Street, New York, New York 10014

British Library Cataloguing-in-Publication Data
A catalogue record for this book is available on
request from the British Library

ISBN: 978 1 78211 997 5
Export ISBN: 978 1 78211 998 2

Typeset in Janson
Designed by Elke Sigal

Printed and bound in Great Britain by Clays Ltd, St Ives plc.

Some names and identifying characteristics have been changed
to protect the privacy of the individuals involved.

The killed object, from which I am separated through sacrifice, while it links me to God, also sets itself up in the very act of being destroyed as desirable, fascinating, and sacred.

JULIA KRISTEVA, *Powers of Horror*

ONCE WE WERE SISTERS

PROLOGUE

IT IS FIFTEEN YEARS BEFORE MANDELA BECOMES PRESIDENT, and South Africa, a country I left at seventeen, is still in the grip of apartheid. It is my thirty-eighth year. It is October, which the Afrikaners call *die mooiste maand*, the prettiest month, our spring.

My mother calls with the news. My brother-in-law, a heart surgeon and protégé of Christiaan Barnard, the first doctor to transplant a human heart successfully, has managed to drive his car off a deserted, dry road and into a lamppost. Wearing his seat belt, he has survived, but my sister was not so lucky. Her ankles and wrists were broken on impact. "She died instantly," my mother assures me. I wonder how one knows such a thing and think of that moment of terror in the dark.

I take a plane out to Johannesburg and go straight to the morgue. I am not sure why I feel I must do this. Perhaps I cannot believe my only sister, not yet forty years old, the mother of six young children, is dead. Perhaps I believe the sight of her familiar face and body will make it clear. Or perhaps I just want to be beside her, to hold her one last time in my arms.

I stand waiting with my hands on the glass, looking into the bright, bare, empty room with the sloping floor made of reddish stone, which dips slightly in the center to provide drainage from the dissection table. Then they wheel her body in. I cannot touch her, hold her, comfort her. I cannot ever heal her. Her whole body is wrapped in a white sheet, only her flower-face tilted up toward me: the broad forehead, the small, dimpled chin, the slanting eyes, the waxy skin. It is my face, our face, the face of our common ancestors. It is the heart-shaped face she would turn up to me obediently when, as children, we played the game of Doll.

This moment is the beginning of endless years of yearning and regret. It is also the beginning of my writing life. Again and again, I will turn to the page to recapture this moment, my sister's life, and her spirit.

With her death, too, comes a flood of questions. How could we have failed to protect her from him? What was wrong with our family? Was it our mother? Our father? Was it our nature, the way we were made, our genes, what we had inherited? Or, more terrible still, is there no answer to such a question? Was it just chance, fate, our stars, our destiny? It was not as if we did not see this coming. What held us back from taking action, from hiring a bodyguard for her? Was it the misogyny inherent in the colonial and racist society in the South Africa of the time? Was it the Anglican Church school where she and I prayed daily that we might forgive even the most egregious sin? Was it the way women were considered in South Africa and in the world at large?

I am still looking for the answers.

I

❦

SNOW

IT IS SNOWING, THE BIG DAMP FLAKES FALLING QUIETLY, strangely, on the dark fir trees, when my sister first mentions the name of the man who will be responsible for her death: Carl. We are in New Haven, Connecticut, in the new tall apartment building, University Towers, where my first baby is born. My husband, a student at Yale, is twenty-one years old. My sister, Maxine, two years older than me, is twenty-two. She has come to be with me for the birth.

We watch my new baby suck on my breast and the snow fall slowly from a ghostly sky with equal wonder. My sister and I are not used to new babies or snow.

Crossways.

11

TOGETHER

We are born in South Africa and grow up together in an L-shaped Herbert Baker house, called Crossways, in Dunkeld, a suburb of Johannesburg. Pale jacarandas line the long allée that leads up to our creeper-covered house. The thick walls and closed shutters keep the rooms cool in the hot afternoons. The vast property, with its swimming pool and fish ponds, a tennis court, a nine-hole golf course, an orchard and vegetable garden, and acres of wild veld stretches out to the blue hills.

An army of servants keeps up the estate. Servants roll the butter between wooden slats with serrated surfaces until it forms small balls that are placed in shell-shaped silver dishes; they polish the silver, the furniture, the floors; they cook the roast beef and Yorkshire pudding, the two green vegetables and the roast potatoes; they simmer the inferior boys' meat ("boys" being how we refer to our adult male servants) into a delicious-smelling stew; they stand in their thin white gloves, their soft silent sandshoes, and starched suits, a bright sash going slantwise across their chests, as they move behind the Chippendale chairs to serve dinner; they go out into the back patio to stoke the coal fire.

Sometimes gangs of convicts are brought in to dig and smooth out the lawns with heavy rollers, to weed the flower beds planted with bright cannas, foxgloves, and nasturtiums. My sister and I stand, holding hands, staring at the men in their striped shirts, their feet bare, digging with the evening light behind them. We listen as they sing in sad harmony before we are told not to stare, to move along, *move along, girls.*

We are always together in the pale green nursery where we sleep with our nanny—the blackboard along one wall and along the other side, the three beds, each with its green bedspread, a wooden bedside cupboard, and a round enamel chamber pot. We are together in the sun-filled breakfast room, where we swallow the thick porridge, the boiled mutton with caper sauce, the Marmite sandwiches with hot milk tea, the heavy English food that makes us sweat; we are together in the corridor with the *Cries of London* lining the wall—the series of prints showing nineteenth-century city vendors calling out their wares—and in the shadowy pantry with the pull-out bins for flour and cornmeal and the big bags of oranges that perfume the air.

We are together in the sunshine in our identical smocked dresses, our sandals, our fair bare heads. We have identical Airedales, Dale and Tony, two big dogs with the same soft fluffy light-brown fur, who are not allowed into the house, but who roll around with us on the lawn and sleep in their kennels outside in the garden.

Together my sister and I explore the vast garden. We are left to roam in the sunshine, often barefoot, free to dream. We know all the flowers and trees intimately like the familiar characters in a favorite book.

They are part of our games, our imagination. They are half real, half made-up, part of our fantasies and our reality, our transitional objects.

We smash mulberries on our faces for war paint and play Cowboys and Indians. We climb the jacaranda trees. They are all good except for the last one on the left, which is wicked, and which we avoid assiduously. We set up a pulley between our respective trees and send it back and forth with little notes written to one another, though I cannot yet read or write properly, and we can call out to one another much more easily.

Maxine and me in the garden at Crossways.

We make up our own secret language, a complicated system of spelling backward: "cat" is "tac," though there are few words I can spell, and I keep forgetting the rules.

We give our identical dolls swimming lessons, tying string around their rubber waists and dragging them up and down the pool, instructing them to kick. We lie on the concrete around the pool in the sunshine and play the game of Touching Tongues, giggling. A bee stings me while we are doing this, and our nanny tells us this is what happens to naughty girls.

I sit in front with my sister behind me, her legs around my waist, using our hands as paddles sailing around the big enamel bath, with its claws for feet, visiting foreign countries, going "overseas," traveling around and around, splashing the water on the black-and-white-tiled floor.

We whisper together in the shadows in the back of the nanny's square green Chevrolet. "Let's make a bunch," I say, and together we slip off the seat, crouch down, and strain, producing a small malodorous gift for the nanny. We run down to hide in the bottom of the garden, terrified at our wickedness.

We climb the stile and hide down in the wild part of the garden, listening to the wind in the swaying bamboo. We play the secret game of Doll. Alternately Maxine is the "doll,"

———————————— ❧ ————————————

lying stiff and obedient to my wishes, or the mistress, who makes me do whatever she wants me to do.

It is this game I think of later, when the Roman men call out to us, "*Che bambola!*" What a doll!, and much later still, when I see my sister, her shattered body wrapped in white as in swaddling clothes.

III

FIRST GLIMPSES

In New Haven my sister holds my new baby girl up in the air and admires her dark slanting eyes. Maxine says she is beautiful. She props the baby's head over her shoulder and pats her back and tells me about the man she has just met, who wants to marry her.

We have both laughed at, flirted with, and danced with many different boys.

In Johannesburg we were known as the Kohler girls: Maxine, the elder one, the sweet one, with her soft blond curls and long-lashed violet eyes, her pale delicate skin that bruises so easily, the shy smile; and Sheila May, two years younger, darker-skinned, with straight hair, gray-green sloe eyes, and narrow, boyish hips.

Maxine is the one who never suffers from spots, the one

who is said to look "like an English rose." She is dreamy, good-natured, and merry. Her kindness does not mask her intelligence, but it is obvious her sympathy comes first. She seems placid, but as with a calm sea on a sunny day there are sudden squalls.

I torment her in the nursery by touching her bed with the tip of my finger, which I know annoys her. I lean across from my bed and poke. "Please don't touch my bed," she says again and again, "*please* don't touch my bed," and finally, when I continue to laugh and touch the bed, she throws the glass of juice she is drinking in my face.

When we fight as children in the back of the car, Mother suggests we both get boxing gloves.

"I hate her," I tell Mother in a rage.

"No, you don't, you love her," Mother says.

I do, I do.

Maxine laughs and cries easily, her big eyes quick to fill with tears at a glimpse of someone else's sorrow. She will pick up someone else's baby on the beach, if it is crying. She is the musical one, the one who learns the Mozart sonatas and plays with feeling, the one who gets the Steinway, when Mother takes it out of storage. When I try to play nursery rhymes to my children on the piano, they will run away.

We are both readers, curious about people, the past, and above all, about love.

Now Maxine holds my baby, Sasha, in the Viyella night-dress with the drawstring neck, that my mother and sister have brought into my small room in the Grace–New Haven Hospital in a carry-cot filled with clothes for my baby to wear. She tells me about the young doctor she has met in Johannesburg. I am not sure how much she tells me that day, or even how I react to her words. I am unaware of their importance in our lives. I am preoccupied with my new husband, my new baby, and with the blood that flows from my own body. Much later, her children will fill in the blanks with words that ring with significance.

She has caught a first glimpse of Carl at a tennis party in Johannesburg. He is playing tennis, hitting the ball hard in the sunshine. She finds him dashing in his tennis whites and is, her son later tells me, "immediately smitten at the sight."

At twenty I have already married the American I first glimpsed at nineteen standing in the shadows outside our ground-floor flat in Rome. He was slouching slightly in the dim light, before the iron gate in the Parioli. A long, lanky twenty-year-old with high cheekbones and a blond forelock that tumbled into his slanting eyes, he was slim-hipped in his blue jeans, the white shirtsleeves turned up to the bony elbows. He was ringing our bell in Rome. I stood hesitating in the twilight, my hand on the ornate wrought-iron gate.

IV

SUITORS

Now Maxine tells me she, too, is thinking of marrying.
"But what's he like?" I ask.

He is a blond and blue-eyed Afrikaner who grew up in
Ermelo, a small town in the Transvaal, and his father works
as a superintendent on the railways, or perhaps she says he
is a caretaker of gardens. He seems to like flowers. Carl's
mother's name is Azalea, which does not suit her at all, I will
think, when I meet her years later. There is nothing flower-
like about Ouma, as we will call her—using the Afrikaans
name for *grandmother*—a large, solid lady with a heavy
hand. Her youngest son, Louis, will say much later that his
mother tried with increasing bitterness to get her children
to continue to speak Afrikaans by taking them to the Dutch

Reformed Church, something they resisted. English has become their language, the language of what Ouma probably considers the oppressor.

Carl, a nerd at school with thick-rimmed glasses, one of his daughters will tell me later, had been teased as a boy. He passed his matriculation at sixteen and is already a doctor at twenty-one.

"I don't think he's had time to read Dostoyevsky," Maxine says and laughs.

My sister and I have sworn we will never marry anyone who has not read Dostoyevsky. We have copied out long passages from Ivan Karamazov's speeches about the existence of evil in the world into our black hardback notebooks.

"And what about James and Tom and Neville Rosser?" I ask. She laughs and strokes the soft fair fluff on my baby's round head.

I know my sister, at twenty-two, has seriously considered several suitors: James, a good-natured South African who owns a large banana farm with blue trees and many big dogs in Natal; Tom, a slim, fair Scot with curly hair, who wants to become an Anglican priest; and Neville Rosser, who took her to the school dance, and who has glossy black hair, a dimple in his chin, and will become an engineer and even find oil in his backyard, I find out later.

❧

Then there is Henry, the distinguished Englishman, the member of the Grenadier Guards, the son of a friend of Mother's who took Maxine out the night of her presentation to the Queen, she tells me.

My sister dropped a curtsy before the Queen in a pale mauve, pleated dress with a décolleté that showed off her smooth young skin, and a little mauve pillbox hat that perched on the back of her blond curls.

Mother, who is friendly with the wife of the South African ambassador to England, Harry Andrews, had my sister's presentation arranged, though Mother's accountant, a Mr. Perks, who manages our money, protested. He considered a presentation to the Queen would encourage her to "live above her station."

My mother, like many white South African women, rarely speaks of politics, hardly reads the newspaper, or only the kind with headlines like "Monkey Steals Baby from Carriage," but anything about the English royal family, on the contrary, has an almost sacred glow. She reveres the Queen, who has been so brave, she says, during the war, the Queen who will become the Queen Mother in 1952.

We were even taken to see the royal family, including the two princesses, in 1947, Princesses Elizabeth and Margaret, when they came out to South Africa for a visit. I remember the crush of the crowds and a terrible moment, when my sister let go of my hand, and I was lost for a few moments of panic.

I still have a photograph of Maxine in her presentation dress on my bedroom wall, and sometimes people ask me if it is a photo of me, which makes my heart tilt with sorrow. There is something so unworldly about her with the cloud of light behind her head, a misty English countryside suggested in the background. She sits there in her ethereal loveliness in her pale mauve dress with the pleats, a curl on her forehead, her shy smile. Why did I not sense she would escape us all? Why did I not see how soon this would be, and how tragic?

I remember how my sister told me Prince Phillip, poor man, looked very bored at this endless procession of young girls, peered down the front of her décolleté to get a glimpse of her smooth breasts.

After the presentation she was asked out by this young Englishman who invited her to his flat. At his door she made the embarrassing error in etiquette of shaking hands with his batman, a sort of superior servant of an officer, she tells me.

She has told all these suitors she will make up her mind soon. Now she has met someone new, which adds to her confusion. She often has difficulty making up her mind.

Maxine in her presentation dress.

"Mummy's against it," my sister says, smiling ruefully. She holds my little girl so lovingly against her shoulder, her hand on her head. My sister loves babies.

"Why? A handsome doctor, and you always said you wanted to be a doctor yourself," I say.

"Well, the Afrikaans background, though he speaks perfect English—and you know what she thinks of them, going around saying they beat the natives with a *sjambok* and commit incest on their deserted farms."

Mother maintains her grandfather was a Russian nobleman, whose land was usurped by a wicked uncle. He had to leave his vast estate, his serfs, the forests of white birch, and flee his country. He wandered through many lands, learning the twelve languages, not including the native ones, which he supposedly spoke. Passing through Salonika, he adopted the name of the place and came out to South Africa. I will later discover he started a grocery store there, though Mother leaves this less-glamorous part out of her story.

Was he perhaps a Greek? I wonder, later in my life, seeing the picture of the dark-haired merchant, standing outside his store, his apron tied around his waist, surrounded by his large family. Wherever her family came from, Mother looks down on the Afrikaners, the Boers. She considers them uncouth and, though she herself has never finished high school, uneducated. She makes fun of their simple guttural language and cites their translations from the Bible with derision. She maintains the Afrikaans translation of "Gird up your loins" is "*Maak vas jou broek,*" which makes her laugh because of the sound of the simple words. Since the bitter Anglo-Boer War at the start of the twentieth century, there has remained great enmity between the two white tribes.

My sister says the family is quite poor. Carl is the only one who seems to have succeeded so brilliantly, thanks to a good brain, a capacity to focus on the task at hand, and hard work. There are innumerable brothers and sisters, and a niece will later tell me his mother, Azalea, would run after them and beat them all hard with a hairbrush.

"The mother is rather plump and wears terrible hats. You know what a snob Mummy can be," Maxine says.

"Do you love him?" I ask.

"I like how frank he is with me, that he tells me the truth, says what he thinks. It's refreshing," she says.

"I know what you mean," I say, smiling at her, thinking of how we have both scoffed at all those "nice" boys our mother has introduced us to, all seemingly called Cecil or Montague. We don't give much weight to Mother's opinion on the subject of marriageable men, or indeed on anything else. On the contrary, we are open to others, ready to take a chance. We both know that Mother, who has not had the privileged childhood we have had, nor the education, feels it is important to marry someone wealthy and live in a large house with many servants as she has been able to do.

When I tell Mother I would like to be independent, to find meaningful work, she stares at me blankly and says with genuine surprise, "What on earth would you want to work for, dear?" Much of her life has been a successful struggle to avoid any work.

V

TOKOLOSH

MOTHER LIVES THE LAZY LIFE OF THE PRIVILEGED WHITE woman in apartheid South Africa. She spends her mornings sipping tea, dressing up. She sallies forth in her flowered hat, gloves, and high heels to visit friends or to shop in Rosebank, a suburb of Johannesburg. She spends our father's hard-earned money. He, twenty years older than her, does not seem to mind, though from time to time he says, "Money does not grow on trees," and appears briefly in the evenings, going through the garden turning off taps.

Mother buys innumerable pastel dresses, leghorn hats with flowers, and pale kid gloves with buttons up to the elbow for herself, for her two sisters, her friends. She buys shoes; she has many pairs of small, delicate, expensive European shoes.

She and her sisters are proud of their small hands and feet, their soft dark curls, their hazel eyes. Appearances are most important; they are what has enabled her to advance: the clothes, the figure, the face. "Clothes maketh the man," she says. Sometimes, unexpectedly, though she cannot spell, she quotes Shakespeare.

She has the nanny dress us up in smocked dresses, organdy sunsuits with little sleeves like wings, white socks, and shoes.

Above all, Mother sleeps. She grasps sleep greedily in her clenched fists, as though it were the most precious thing in the world. She sleeps all through the long hot afternoons in the green light of her high-ceilinged room with the shutters drawn down, one arm flung with abandon across her face, her dark curls clinging to her damp forehead.

And she drinks. She starts drinking at sundown on the glassed-in veranda, surrounded by her two sisters and younger brother, while the blue hills disappear in the dim light.

Holding up her empty crystal glass, Mother says, "Will you get me the other half, Pie?" Pie, the eldest of her three sisters, who is two years older than my mother and a little taller, jumps up obediently to bring Mother another drink and after that, another one.

We learn there are many "other halves," in this whole, as many as she desires. None of her family, who are all dependent on her and my father's money, will even try to stop her. Her two sisters do her bidding.

She is the middle one, the one they call Bill, because she was a tomboy. She is the lucky one, she says, the only one who has married a wealthy man, a hardworking timber merchant. There is a brother, too, whom they call Proie, but he does not seem to count or amount to much.

It is a world of women who obey Mother.

"I have to wee," Mother says to my Aunt Pie, whose real name is Dorothy, but whom she calls Pie, perhaps a shortened form of Sweetie Pie.

"That's one thing I can't do for you," Pie says with a thin smile.

Occasionally the youngest one of our aunts, Hazel, the one who is considered the cleverest, who has worked for a while as some sort of secretary, who knows how to spell, dares to say what she thinks.

As my sister and I are sitting in the back of Mother's Jaguar, and she prepares to drive us home after a party, Aunt Hazel puts her head in the car window and says, "You shouldn't drive with children in the car in the state you are in, Bill!" Mother purses her lips with disgust. "How can she talk to me like that?" Mother says, driving off, weaving slowly, dangerously, down the road.

———————————— ❧ ————————————

"Light me a cigarette, Pet," Mother says, and I am obliged to climb forward and push in the cigarette lighter to light up her Craven A, which makes me feel sick.

Sometimes Mother changes. We do not understand what has happened to her. It is one of Mother's secrets, of the many mysteries that surround her.

She becomes strange. Gradually she draws away from us into her own foreign world. We watch with increasing terror as her face alters: her mouth becomes thin, turns down at the corners; her words are slurred and almost unintelligible. She speaks another thick thorny language, difficult to pronounce; her gestures alter; she staggers; she walks stiffly in an attempt at a straight line.

We fear a witch has come and taken Mother's place, and we are not sure Mother will come back to us. This could happen to anyone, this terrifying metamorphosis. Worst of all, we fear this could happen to us.

Once, lying side by side in our beds in the dark, we see a light glimmering in the big bay window in the nursery.

"It's the Tokolosh," I say. I am certain an evil spirit, what the Zulus call the Tokolosh, has come for us, to take us away. We lie still, unable to move, to call out.

Our nanny teaches us to kneel by our beds, press our hands together, and pray:

Matthew, Mark, Luke, and John,
Bless the bed that I lie on.
Four corners to my bed,
Four angels 'round my head;
One to watch and one to pray
And two to bear my soul away.

V I

TALK

WHILE WE TALK, THE JANUARY SNOW STILL FALLS SOFTLY outside the sliding glass door, which opens onto a narrow terrace in New Haven. We remain together, my sister and I, in the low-ceilinged living room of the new apartment in University Towers that my husband and I have rented. My sister and I are not used to the cold, have no idea how to dress for weather of this kind, and imagine the baby would freeze outside, so we stay inside in the overheated rooms.

Michael and I have filled them with an odd mix of faux-Spanish antiques and Scandinavian furniture, which we have bought on weekends in New York at Bloomingdale's.

An only child with divorced parents, he is eager to make a home. His father, Michael tells me, carried a card to attest to his membership in the Russian aristocracy, but was a man of

---

modest means. He worked at Macy's as a buyer of fine watches, but lived like a wealthy man with an apartment on Park Avenue and a stone house, which he called his dacha, in New Canaan. Though it has long since been sold, Michael proudly shows me the photographs. He went to Europe every summer to buy watches for Macy's and stayed in the best hotels. He "borrowed from Peter to pay Paul," he has told his boy. He married four times, though the last one was not a real marriage, apparently.

Both his father and his Southern mother, who is the poor cousin in a wealthy family of horse owners from Lexington, Kentucky, have been preoccupied above all by keeping up appearances. She now lives with an Italian lover, a count who has no money. "Count No-Account," she says. Both his parents have been trying above all to make ends meet, while pretending to be rich. Michael, consequently, would like to fill our first home with lovely things.

My sister sits on the sofa with its carefully chosen lily pattern and rocks my baby girl. She sings Brahms's Lullaby for her in her sweet voice.

"Lullaby and good night, sleep, my little one, softly," my sister sings to my sleeping child. "Close your eyes, la-la-la, you are Mother's delight." While my baby sleeps, my husband, Michael, attends his classes in French literature at the university, which accepts only young men. It is 1962.

I have tried to talk to his classmates about Plato's *Sympo-*

sium, a book I am reading. It is about a drinking party where each of the men speaks in praise of love, but Michael's friends look at me askance: A pregnant woman without a university degree, talking about Plato? What could she know? It is apparently something they cannot grasp. They turn the conversation back to cooking, babies.

Maxine sits by the big window and holds my new baby and talks about Carl. She tells me she has had a call from one of his old girlfriends.

"Who was she?" I ask.

"A tall, attractive girl with the name of a bright flower," Maxine says pensively. "Strelizia, she said her name was."

The girl telephoned and asked if she might come and talk to my sister. She wanted to tell her something very important.

"What did she say?" I ask.

"It's so strange. She begged me not to marry him," my sister tells me, looking at me.

"Why not?" I ask.

"She would not tell me why. She just kept saying, 'You *must* not marry him. Do you understand? I can't tell you why not, but believe me, *please* believe me, you must not marry him.'"

"What a strange thing to say," I say uneasily.

"I presume she must just be jealous or something. Perhaps she wants to marry him herself," my sister says, stroking her long, doll-like dark lashes between finger and thumb.

———————————————— ❧ ————————————————

"Do you think so?" I ask.

It is only later that the significance of this comes back to me, and I wish with all my heart that the woman had had the courage to explain what she really meant. What dark secrets had she already discovered? Why did she not dare to tell my sister what she knew? What did she fear?

So many things not said, not known.

VII

KNOWLEDGE

Yet it is my sister who knows all I believe as a child.

It is she who has the knowledge. I follow her around, her pale shadow, pretending to do what she does, "reading" a book, *Pinocchio*, because she, two years older than me, is reading it. "You are not reading, silly," she says, laughing at me.

"I am!" I say, holding the book upside down, sitting on the soft velvet sofa in the dimness of the lounge, with the soft mauve carpet, and the mauve velvet curtains closed on the light.

I stay in the swimming pool as long as she and my cousin do. I tread water, though my teeth are chattering with cold, my lips blue, my fingers crinkled like an old woman's.

I imitate and emulate as long as she will permit it. Sometimes she escapes me. She vanishes.

---❦---

Once, we are told to take our afternoon nap in the nursery with our cousin Heather, Pie's daughter, who is four years older than I am and often spends time with us. When I awake, I discover my sister and my cousin had only pretended to lie down to sleep, and while I was sleeping, they slipped out quietly and went off to swim at the public swimming pool, leaving me to wake up alone in the nursery. I feel this departure is a terrible betrayal; they have lied to me, left me alone. I weep bitterly.

My sister is the only one allowed into my father's study, a mysterious place on the west side of the house. I have peeped in there and seen the fat, dark leather armchairs, the big desk before the window, the gramophone, where I believe little men must live and make music. Maxine is allowed into this sanctum sanctorum to file Father's papers, a mysterious operation that concerns the alphabet, which I do not yet know.

We rarely see my father, who leaves before we wake up, slipping off silently, driven down the driveway in his shiny Rolls-Royce, going to the timber yard, where he makes all our money.

Once, though, by chance, I saw him standing naked in the black-and-white-tiled bathroom before the big basin, and I dared to go up to him and touch the thing dangling there temptingly like a bell. I reached up and said, "Ding

My father's Rolls-Royce coming in the gate at Crossways.

---

dong!," swinging it back and forth with my little fingers, much to his ire.

Maxine will be the one to explain the strange secrets of sex to me. We are walking together on the dry lawn—it is winter in the Highveld, and the grass is yellow and stiff. She tells me how the man puts his part into the woman to make a baby.

"It's not true!" I exclaim.

"But it is. Cross my heart," she says.

At the thought of this absurdity I fall to the grass and roll around in laughter, holding my stomach. For some reason this seems extraordinarily funny to me.

My sister says severely, "There is nothing funny about it at all!"

VIII

WEDDINGS

I DO NOT GO TO MY SISTER'S WEDDING IN JOHANNESBURG, though she has come to mine. There are so many times in her short life when I have let her down, betrayed her, when she has called out to me, and I have refused to respond. Once, much later, she comes to America with her children and rents a beautiful yacht on Chesapeake Bay. She telephones me in Connecticut, where we are spending the summer, and asks me to join her. "Please come," she says, but I refuse, so preoccupied with my own paltry problems, my own obsessions, and my own husband. Perhaps, too, I need to see the world through other eyes, eyes that are no longer hers.

Why was I not at her wedding? I do not remember the reason I gave my only sister. Was it because I had let myself be carried along entirely by my husband, like a leaf caught

—————————————— ❧ ——————————————

up in the current of a strong river, buoyed up by his needs and desires?

Was it because my husband did not want to confront this crowd of relatives and friends, who had repeatedly told him on his wedding day what a lucky man he was to marry me? Was he obliged to pass an examination that day, and did he wish to have me at his side? Or was it that I was glad that part of me had escaped this old world of my childhood, my relatives, my mother, even my sister, and entered a new, brash American world? Instead I sent a telegram wishing that the bells would ring harmoniously. Maxine responded saying they had, indeed. Perhaps they had.

Yet Maxine stood behind me as a bridesmaid at my wedding like a white shadow. All the bridesmaids were in white. She followed me up the aisle, as I had followed her as a child around the garden, doing whatever she did, as I will wish to follow her into death. When I accepted the ring, she held my bouquet for me, as she would later hold my baby. There was no engagement ring. How could this twenty-one-year-old boy produce such a thing?

I walked up to the altar in the Anglican stone church, St. Martin's-in-the-Veld, in Johannesburg on my uncle's arm, wearing a white silk dress, my breasts swelling suspiciously beneath the smooth cloth.

A saleswoman who fitted me with a new bra for my trousseau said, "I hope you don't mind me saying so, but you have beautiful breasts." I did not tell her the reason for the sweet swell. The Greek dressmaker, Mme. Vlamos, who seemed to get herself into all the wedding photos, was one of the only people who was alerted to the predicament.

I held a bouquet of lily of the valley in my hands, and I wept.

What about my dreams of being a writer, a teacher? What about my education? As children, my sister and I had laid the crayons out before us and pretended they were our pupils.

Pregnant, I married this boy who had finally penetrated my body, a few months before, in Paris.

At nineteen or twenty, I was still a child, lingering on in the imaginary world I was accustomed to, a world of nineteenth-century books, a child's world of fantasies. I was in a story, as I will be all my life to some extent. A subterranean stream of story runs parallel with reality through all my life.

I was there but also on the page in words that conjured up a fiction. At nineteen, the reality of a masculine body with its frightening parts was too threatening to me. I felt inadequate, not ready for the reality of his hard, dangerous, thrusting sex.

Michael wrote in despair to his mother at his lack of success, and she had her Italian lover reply with kind words of advice and encouragement. Enzo was a kind man. "It has happened to me many times," Enzo said, perhaps not quite understanding the situation.

Finally, one evening, on the bed in his apartment in the Latin Quarter in Paris, Michael did manage to penetrate my reluctant body. There was no blood, no pain, no ecstasy. Afterward he played Ray Charles, and I retreated to the bath, flushing out the semen as best as I could, and then leaving in an unreasonable rage, slamming the door. Though I allowed this to happen, did nothing to stop him except to present him with my stiff, unyielding body, somewhere within myself I felt deeply and irrevocably violated.

I spent the night in a hotel room, while he wandered the streets, looking for me. I wrote two letters that night: one to an old German boyfriend, Richard, who had always respected my virginity, describing the scene, which seemed to me like two frogs copulating; and I wrote a letter to Michael, but somehow I sent the wrong letter to the wrong man. It was Michael who read about the frogs. Obviously, I was angry with this determined young man, who was struggling with his own demons, a man whom I married in my white silk dress, a man to whom I would give my heart.

My sister, whom I followed around so faithfully as a child, now follows in my footsteps, though she is the older one, and her choice seems so much wiser: a doctor at twenty-one, a brilliant boy, who will study to be a cardiothoracic surgeon. He will learn to be good with hearts, so to speak. Out there, they are often good with hearts. They take a heart

❦

from the almost stiff and put it into the barely quick. He will tell us that the difficulty is not so much exchanging hearts as finding the right ones to exchange.

Carl seems a much more suitable choice of husband than my own, Michael, who is a lanky boy who looks so much like me, that people inquire if we are brother and sister. He is a boy without fortune, who is still a student at university, studying French literature and political science.

It was even suggested to me by the accountant, Mr. Perks, that instead of marrying him I go quietly to Europe with one of my aunts and give up my baby for adoption. Instead, I married but lost the baby almost immediately, once we were back in Paris in the apartment on Rue de Noisiel, with the blue walls and the one pink azalea plant, the blood flowing from me through the night while the two cats, Kochka and Minette, slept on my bed.

We would make a new baby almost immediately. I am like the Japanese man in a film I will see in later years, *The Woman in the Dunes*, who falls into a deep dune and is trapped down there, obliged to remain with a woman who must dig the sand endlessly. When he finally has the chance to escape, he no longer has the desire to leave her.

Maxine marries in the same stone church where I married Michael.

When I ask Libby Paul, one of the bridesmaids, what she

remembers about the wedding and the reception, she tells me that, above all, she remembers that she was the one who recommended the dressmaker, as she was doing some modeling for her. Also, apparently there was not enough material, a Thai wild silk, for all the bridesmaids' dresses, so they were made in different shades. In the black-and-white photo, which is all I see, they all look white.

At my sister's wedding Mother seems mollified, though she complains about Ouma's hat. Carl's mother wears a rather odd-looking bonnet for the wedding, which I see in the photographs, and which reminds me of the red bonnets men wore in the eighteenth century during the French Revolution.

Mother moves into a comfortable cottage in the grounds of the couple's big house on Valley Road. Roses grow outside her bay window, and there is an extra bedroom for my Aunt Pie, who moves in with her.

Carl will work as a doctor in Johannesburg: an esteemed and energetic young man with a finely chiseled face, a hard knotty body, the sudden flash of an unexpected white smile. He is tall, blond, and athletic. His nurses adore him, Maxine tells me; his grateful patients speak highly of his postoperative care, he does pro bono work on the weekends, even flies to Lesotho to operate there. His large family—several brothers and sisters; an intelligent mother, despite the hats, who is of distinguished French Huguenot stock; a father who, though

Maxine and Carl's wedding with Ouma and Oupa
and my mother in the wide-brimmed hat.

not wealthy, seems responsible and kind—all look up to him, the brilliant *boetie*, the one who has passed his matriculation at sixteen, the one who will go on to Edinburgh to do his special training in heart surgery, the one who works with Christiaan Barnard at Groote Schuur, though not on the first famous heart transplant, but later and, particularly, on a difficult operation with a man whose heart seems to stop completely before starting up again.

My sister will soon fill the rooms of her big house with babies. She tells me her South African gynecologist encourages her in this endeavor. "We need more white babies," he says.

IX

NAMES

Our mother has her two white babies, her two little girls, one named after my father, Max, and one after her, Sheila May. I understand that my father loves my sister more. She is older and knows more than I do and can talk with my brilliant father during his brief appearances. Maxine knows how to read and write, how to add, subtract, and multiply, and how to file his papers. She is his preferred one. In a photo of the four of us on the beach she sits at his feet and leans longingly up against his legs. Because of her name, Maxine, I feel she is part of him, a little Max. They belong together.

Once, we are taken to the timber yard to see our father and tumble around in the sawdust, which goes down the backs of our dresses and pricks our necks. We are introduced to one of Father's employees, who tells us that when Maxine was born, he put a gold coin in her hand, which she grasped greedily.

As sometimes happens in families, there is a pairing here; my sister is my father's "Pet," as I am my mother's, or so I understand. Later, my sister's children will tell me Maxine thought she was Mother's "Pet."

Sometimes, in the mornings, when our father has left the house, Mother allows both her little pets to enter her big bedroom, the lined curtains drawn on the bright light. We climb up into her wide, soft bed with the initialed blue linen sheets. She gathers us up to her bosom, almost visible through the sheer pink nylon nightgown.

She permits us to slip our hands into the dark at the back of the secret drawer in her kidney-shaped dressing table with the triple mirror, the glass top, and the sea-green organdy skirt, where she hides her jewels. We bring forth the Craven A tin. She tips out the bright snakes of tangled necklaces and bracelets onto the blue sheets. She decks us out with her rings and brooches. She slips her brilliant diamonds, the yellow, the brown, the blue, and the blue-white, into our hair, and onto our fingers and toes. She dances us on her knees. She sings, "And she shall have music wherever she goes."

X

PREGNANCY

WE ARE BOTH PREGNANT NOW, MY SISTER WITH HER FIRST baby boy, me with my second, fifteen months after the first. Michael hopes for a boy.

My sister, who started her university studies of languages at the University of Cape Town, graduates from Wits, the University of the Witwatersrand, in Johannesburg. It is 1963.

I have a graduation photograph of her with my mother in her wide-brimmed hat and pearls and my Aunt Hazel with her dark curls, at her side. They are standing smiling proudly in the sunshine. Look how happy they seem! Maxine is pregnant, her stomach swelling in her graduation robe, as she holds a scroll in her hand, a black band around her neck.

Without any degree and dressed in a loose jacket, I slip surreptitiously into the back of darkened auditoriums at Yale. I

Graduation day.

listen to Victor Brombert and Henri Peyre lecture on French literature, and Vincent Scully, on art. With my sleeping child in her stroller, I haunt the Yale art gallery in New Haven. I read all the books Michael reads and coach him with the flash cards I have made for his exams. I coach him for his art exams. I make him identify the pictures of famous paintings, parts of famous paintings, the feet of a girl on a swing. I take notes on the books he is reading and help write his papers. He writes a paper on the mask and the mirror image in the work of Stendhal.

I kneel beside the gray four-poster colonial bed to pray to God for his success during his exams.

It seems we make love in the sunny bedroom every afternoon. I sigh and make the noises I have heard in the films, though the real pleasure will not come until much later. Easily, so easily, so young, healthy, and fertile, we fall pregnant, my sister and me. Our husbands seem to prefer us pregnant. The pill is still controversial, Maxine's gynecologist does not recommend it. It will give you varicose veins, he says.

Both our babies are expected in early May.

In New Haven it turns hot unexpectedly, and I have to buy summer clothes for the few weeks that remain of my maternity. I sit out in a loose pale green cotton dress, my stomach swelling. I sweat on a bench at the edge of the New Haven Green and watch my little girl, Sasha, play in the grass. It seems the new baby will never come.

I sit at my huband's new Scandinavian desk in the dim light of the dawn in the living room at University Towers with the bookcases behind me. I talk to my sister in Johannesburg on the telephone in the early morning, Sasha on my lap.

"How are you? How did it go?" I inquire about the birth. Her baby has arrived earlier than expected. All has gone well, she tells me. She has a beautiful baby boy whom they will call Vaughan.

My baby, who was supposed to arrive before my sister's, is the laggard. She is taking her sweet time, reluctant to leave me. She tarries, while my sister's boy is in more of a hurry to come into the world. The doctor decides finally to induce the birth. Cybele, my second child, a big baby girl, arrives two weeks late. Mother sends my Aunt Pie to help with the new baby and the long flight with the two small children from New York to Milan to meet my sister and her new baby. We are on the way to Rapallo. Pie is wonderful with babies and wraps them up tightly, winding the baby blanket around the little limbs.

XI

VOYAGES

My sister and I are always flying long distances back and forth to meet in beautiful places. We meet in South Africa, travel to the game reserve together with my new husband soon after I marry Michael, laughing at old jokes. We meet in France, and tour the countryside together to study art. We stand in stunned silence in the shadows of ancient Romanesque churches, looking up at the round stone arches with wonder. We travel to England; to Scotland, where Carl is specializing in thoracic surgery; to Switzerland to ski. We go to Greece to visit the Greek temples. We stand on the Acropolis and gaze out at the city below. We travel to Italy with our growing families. We are nomads of a kind. My mother often says, "I feel better when I am moving."

All these visits with my sister over the years in many

———————————— ❧ ————————————

famous places have run together in my mind. They hardly seem real to me. They have become a song, a litany, a sung prayer, its distinct notes chiming mournfully in my mind. Like Mother's words when she tells of her travels with our father, the places ring in my mind repeatedly. "Ah, Banff, Lake Louise," Mother says with a sigh. Or, "Big Sur! Carmel!" reciting the litany of her voyages to people who have never been there.

I see Maxine turning to me, laughing, on a boat, the wind whipping her curls; standing clutching her *Guide Bleu* to her swelling stomach in the shadows of a stone church.

I remember our trips to Zermatt in Switzerland, the children standing together for a photograph with their skis at their sides like spears. I recall the long arduous voyages out to South Africa with small children to visit her in her home in Johannesburg and a trip to Edinburgh, Scotland, where I stay in a hotel room where you have to put money in the meter for heat, and she does the dishes in her fur coat.

This summer, Mother rents a villa on the Ligurian coast near Rapallo on the Italian Riviera, which comes with a cook, Ines, who will remain in our lives, working for both of us at different times.

The villa is on the side of a steep hill with a view of the sea

Maxine and me skiing in Switzerland.

sparkling in the distance. In the early mornings you can hear the chickens clucking in the henhouse, which is halfway down the hill, far enough away so that the noise does not disturb the guests in the rented villa or on the beach. Sometimes at night, the stench rises up in the hot air.

We all arrive in Italy in late June and meet Ines, the cook, who, we will find, has a squint in one eye and likes drama as well as food. She is always blowing up the oven. She is always trying to get Sasha to eat. Sasha seems to have decided, at the birth of her new sister, not to eat. "*Mangia! Mangia!*" Ines urges.

Maxine and Carl arrive with their new baby. The proud father and new mother show us their little boy. We all marvel at this miracle, whom they call "the Professor," because he has a partially bald head. He lies naked on the bed and pees straight up into the air like a Roman fountain. The four of us stand around him and laugh.

Nights, Maxine and I stumble together through the big rooms of the old villa with our new babies in our arms. We wander through the long corridors with the sloping marble floors and the high ceilings and in the distance the soft sound of the sea. We rise in the night, both awake, breast-feeding every three or four hours, and meet in the dim light, whispering and giggling, as we did as girls in the nursery.

My sister sits wearily in her white dressing gown with

her boy baby in a chair by the window at dawn, while I lie on the bed, Cybele's big head on my arm, while we talk about motherhood and the births of our babies.

I tell her so proudly that my baby, at nine and a half pounds, was the biggest one in the hospital. We listen to the chickens clucking and a rooster crowing to announce the day.

We rarely see Carl, who has never been to Europe before and rushes off, thrilled to visit the sights. He falls for Italy at first sight. He seems so energetic, impatient, and enthusiastic, rushing off for day trips from Rapallo to visit Genova, Portofino.

Michael is less enthusiastic about touring. He was dragged through Europe, going from one small hotel room to another with his mother as a little boy. Lonely, unable to sleep, she woke him often in the night just to talk to him.

My mother-in-law is often ill and has sought a cure for her asthma in Switzerland. As a young boy, Michael was sent to Le Rosey, a fancy school for rich boys in Rolle, where they drank wine with their meals. In Rapallo Michael prefers to lie on his bed and read *Jane Eyre*.

My mother scoffs. "A *man* does not read in the morning," she says. Reading is considered an idle pastime, not to be indulged in too frequently. It therefore becomes an illicit source of pleasure.

Our young husbands take an immediate dislike to one

Michael, Sasha, and me in Rapallo.

another, bristling like hostile dogs at first sight. It is clear they have little in common. We seem to have chosen two men at the opposite ends of the spectrum.

Though my sister and I have said we will never marry anyone who has not read Dostoyevsky, Carl has obviously not had much time to read anything but his books on medicine. A poor, bright boy from Ermelo, he has had to work hard, to rip through school as fast as he can. He seems in a great hurry. Ambitious, he knows how to focus on what is essential in his studies.

My sister and I lounge lazily on the terrace of the rented house in light-colored dresses in brief moments of reprieve. The moths hover over the lamps. We are worn out with the nights and days of breast-feeding our babies. We talk nonsense, bring up old jokes, old friends. Maxine laughs easily at our jokes. What I remember above all about her is her light laugh, the touchingly tentative ring of it.

Carl walks up and down restlessly. Beside my sister's ease and naturalness, her good humor, he seems stiff and easily offended, ready to take offense.

My sister wants to know everything; she has a keen sense of what to say and what others are trying to say. She loves people, not in any showy way and not perfectly, but gently, with a wish to please. There is a kind of freedom about her, an acceptance of the foibles and failures of others that Carl, clearly, cannot espouse. His life, we sense, has been filled with narrow rules and regulations, ones he will feel obliged to break but cannot countenance others breaking. He wants, above all, we sense, to be in control. Part of Maxine, he must feel from the start, escapes him.

Carl has not learned the art of conversation at medical school or certainly with us makes little effort to demonstrate what he might have learned. I will discover he knows how to charm when necessary. With us he mostly remains sunk in a sullen silence, unless directly questioned. He glowers. Unlike us he does not take for granted that the world will consider him with benevolence. He buries his unease under a veneer of mockery. His steel-blue eyes flash with impatience. He seems unpredictable, moody, given to sudden bursts of anger that make us nervous, anxious to keep the peace. We placate and appease. We attempt flattery.

Why is he so angry? We do not understand. Is it because his mother beat him with a hairbrush, because the children mocked him at school, or because he, unlike us, has no money? Or is it my sister's ease, her openness, her very love of life that annoys him intensely?

I have the impression he considers us superficial, concerned by appearances. *He* has not spent idle time wandering around a great garden surrounded by servants or learning foreign languages or reading unnecessary books. He gives us the feeling anything we say will be open to censure, cor-rection, or mockery. He seems to say that while we have been wasting our time on stories, he has been studying the essen-tial things of life: the anatomy of the body, the heart and the lungs, the blood pumping through the veins and arteries, life and death.

XII

TRUTH AND FICTION

MY SISTER AND I SIT TOGETHER ON STOOLS, LISTENING TO our mother and our aunts telling stories. Day after day, the three sisters gossip, sitting out in the sunny, glassed-in veranda at Crossways on the wicker furniture that comes from California, beside the big wooden barrel that holds the plants where I once, as did Rousseau, the French philosopher, he confides in his memoirs, dared to pee. They sip morning and afternoon tea and later cocktails, and they talk as fast as they knit. The conversation is accompanied by the click of steel knitting needles, the rhythm, sometimes fast, sometimes slowed to a *moderato cantabile*, by the interest of the words. They have precious leisure time to weave stories while their hands weave a pattern of some sort, knitting like the Fates, crotcheting, or embroidering.

Maxine and me in knitted swimming costumes.

❧

Once they knit us swimming costumes with our initials, MK and SK, embroidered on the chest. When we go into the water, the suits stretch down to our knees.

The three sisters have all had to do fine dressmaking for pocket money as girls on Rocky Street, where they grew up. At Crossways they will lay out their paper patterns on the mahogany dining room table, pinning the pattern to the material, and then cutting with their pinking sheers, the sound of the scissors, like their stories, loud in our ears.

It is talk my sister and I find fascinating.

"Don't go on until I come back," I say, when I have to get up to go to the bathroom, afraid of missing out on some important tidbit of gossip. Occasionally they will say, "Little pitchers have big ears," indicating us children with a glance, but mostly we are allowed to listen freely.

They are all storytellers, and the first stories I am hearing, the ones that fascinate me from the start, are theirs.

They tell the story about a missing girl called Bubbles, who is found half naked in the veld, lying there dead, mud in her blond hair, something stuffed in her mouth. Or is that a story *I* have invented? What is real and what imaginary here? Many years later, a fellow South African will tell me that he, too, puzzled over the account of Bubbles Schroeder in the local newspaper, trying to determine what a "good-time girl" was. Once again, truth is stranger than invention!

Mother, too, seems to find it difficult to make the distinc-
tion. As a little girl, she recounts, she somehow got her head
stuck through the brass bars at the end of her bed. She was
trying to reach, she tells us, the shimmering angel, wings
spread wide, she saw standing at the bottom of her bed in the
morning. I imagine Mother in her white nightdress, stuck,
gazing at a shining angel. She called out desperately, and her
father came running to free her from bondage.

Her father's pet, a fat, willful child, with long black glossy
hair and a big appetite, she was given money to buy new
shoes for school and sent into town on her own. She took the
tram with the money clasped proudly in her plump, sticky
paw. Once there, she walked through the crowded streets,
distracted from her task by the sights, sounds, and above all,
the smells. She smelled baking bread. She stopped and looked
into the window of a bakery and spotted some cream cakes in
the window. She gazed at them longingly. Then she went in
and found the money she had in hand would buy a whole box
of the golden cakes with the cream oozing down the sides.
Irresistible!

Instead of the new shoes for school she spent all her
money on the big box of cream cakes. On the tram going back
to her house on Rocky Street, she ate first one, then two, and
then, unable to stop, she stuffed all of the rest of them into
her mouth. When she got home and her father asked to see

the new shoes, she told him, icing sugar around her mouth, she lost the money in the street.

Mother quotes the odd lines of a poem she says the children would call out to her when she walked down the street: "O fat white lady who nobody loves, / Why do you walk through the fields in white gloves?" I see her walking along, nose in the air, trying to ignore their taunts.

Certainly the three sisters who have grown up together and remained in the same town, who all look alike with their dark curls and their delicate ankles, all know the same people, whose lives they discuss at length and in some fascinating detail.

They all seem in accord, though both Mother and my Aunt Pie, the moment the other walks out of the room, have something critical to say about the other sister. Aunt Pie will say scornfully, when Mother has complained of the worries in her life, "What does she have to worry about, can you tell me!"

And Mother will say, when she gives something to her sister, "I know she'll just give it away to that daughter of hers."

Their stories, I understand, are not entirely what has happened. I sense a selection, an elaboration, exaggeration, dramatization. They choose their facts according to their fancy and restructure them according to their wishes. These are mysterious stories that do not divulge all but carefully hide as much as they reveal. In fact these are stories often told in

The three sisters, Pie in the middle, with
Mother on her left and Hazel on her right.

order to conceal, what Freud, I will later learn, called "screen memories," or so they seem to me, though some of them that seem the most extraordinary and unbelievable will turn out to be true.

The story about our three maiden great-aunts, our grandfather's three sisters, obliged to remain unwed because of their father's will, turns out to be quite true. Their father, afraid of fortune hunters in the early days in the diamond town of Kimberley, stipulated, apparently, in his will that if one of his girls married, all three must forfeit the small fortune, which would then go instead to their cousins. They were thus shackled together forever, a story that would be confirmed by cousins, who sent over suitors in the vain hope of seducing them and thus claiming the fortune.

These are my first stories that I listen to carefully. They will inspire me, and I will use them in my own fiction. I start a novel while sitting on the toilet at five, though I have no memory at all of what it was about. I see myself from a distance in the black-and-white-tiled bathroom at Crossways, leaning forward on the toilet and writing.

I sense the sisters are all good at keeping Mother's secrets, their fictions hiding the mysterious facts of Mother's life from view as much as they reveal them. I will write in an attempt to discover what lies behind these stories.

XIII

DISCOVERIES

In the spring we meet in Greece at a place called Lago-nissi outside Athens. My sister and I visit the Acropolis together. She is pregnant again.

She is interested in archaeology, the digs that have brought forth ancient treasures. She tells me about Schliemann and his discoveries at Mycenae, where Agamemnon slipped on the soaped floor, in one version of his murder by his wife, Clytemnestra, as Agamemnon had sacrificed her daughter, Iphigenia, to the gods.

We both often have books in hand. Between babies we will study at various institutions. We are inquisitive, and different books mark the different moments of our lives.

When my sister dies, she will be reading Jean Rhys's beautiful and tragic *Wide Sargasso Sea*, a friend, who also

Maxine and me at the Acropolis in Athens.
She is holding her guidebook, pregnant again.

---

works in Carl's office, tells me. "Do you think the book influenced her?" the friend asks me. Could this book about Bertha, the foreign wife, the woman who comes from afar, about her childhood and marriage to Mr. Rochester, who shuts her up in the attic, this woman who became the mad wife, have influenced my sister?

"Do you think she might have grabbed the steering wheel away from him, that night in the car?" the friend asks me.

"I certainly don't," I say. "I don't think we can blame this on a book!"

We learn to breast-feed with a baby on an arm and a book in hand. We attend the Sorbonne, the Institut Catholique, the University of Cape Town, Wits, the École du Louvre.

I study French culture at the Sorbonne and eventually the history of art at the Louvre, starting, as the French do, at the beginning, with the first tools used by the first inhabitants, the silex or flints, and going on to the Paleolithic paintings on rocks in caves at places like Lascaux, and rapidly on to a series of overweight Venuses, their generous curves, signs of fertility or perhaps wealth. I get as far as the sixteenth century, when I switch to psychology.

In Greece my elder daughter, Sasha, who is three and a half, teaches herself to swim on the beach in Lagonissi in the shallow waters of the Mediterranean Sea. She learns to lift her feet from the ground and to kick, buoyant and laughing

———————————— ❧ ————————————

in the clear water. We take a boat to visit the islands nearby, including the beautiful island of Hydra.

In a photo the four children are on the beach, my sister's blond boy, Vaughan, and little girl, Lisa, and my two girls, Sasha and Cybele, in their white sun hats, red-checked sun-suits, smiling faces tilted up to the sun.

Cybele, who is two, is already wearing a white bodice with two pockets that carry the heavy receivers of her hearing aids. She totters across the beach, tipping forward like a teapot.

The summer before, during a visit to Italy to see my mother-in-law, who lives there, Michael and I had lain lazily, stretched out in the sun on the beach, listening to the sound of a peddler's voice, crying out his wares: *Canditi qui vuole?* Sweets, who wants them? he cried. His cries came to me like the echo of a thousand summers.

I was just able to see Cybele through my half-shut eyes, playing with her green bucket and spade in the sand. Look what a lovely child she was at eighteen months, crouching down in her blue and white romper, her little fat dimpled knees, her flushed cheeks!

My mother-in-law, long, lean, and elegant like her son, was draped across her deck chair, a cream straw hat pulled down to one side to shade her pale face, her long legs grace-fully tucked to one side. She watched us with her pale perceptive eyes, and then called out to Cybele. "Cybele! Cybele! Cybele!" The child's name with its long vowel sounds seemed to fill the beach with a cadence both wild and sad. Then she clapped her hands loudly in the air. Cybele went on playing with her bucket.

I had noticed that the child had a high-pitched voice, and asked our pediatrician, "Is her voice normal?"

"What is normal?" he had asked, looking at me severely.

My mother-in-law now said in her Southern drawl, "Why, Sheila, do you know, I don't believe that child can hear." I looked at her thinking, *That woman, that woman, she always sees the fly in the ointment.* I got up fast, almost squawking like a mother hen disturbed in her nest. I gathered up my child and carried her down to the sparkling sea, wading into the water and swinging her around and around in the air, her little toes skimming the surface, the glistening drops of water falling from her feet like diamonds, aware, despite myself, that the world would never look quite the same again.

Now, my sister and I eat in an outdoor restaurant in Piraeus with the four children. We look around the big crowded terrace, with its flowers and white tablecloths and elegant Greek people, in wonder. It is a Sunday luncheon and all the well-behaved European children are sitting upright and quiet through the long meal with such patience, obediently eating everything placed before them.

———————————— ❧ ————————————

"What do they do to them?" I ask, leaning across the table toward my sister. Our four children are all under the table, crawling around and throwing bread at one another and laughing.

"What is important with children is to be consistent," my sister says.

Or am I the one who says that?

XIV

DEATH

MANY OF THESE VIVID MEMORIES COME TO ME MUDDLED IN my mind by the fictions I have written about them, shifting the point of view, seeing the story through different eyes. Who says this, my sister or me? Often, we are comingled in my mind, as fiction blends with fact. Fiction or simply the writing down of the story has replaced reality, another loss. Objects are what remain most clearly in my mind, the indisputable details.

When we are seven and nine, our parents leave us for eighteen months to go on an around-the-world trip to buy timber. They go to Europe, Scandinavia, South and North America, by ship, rail, and car. This is 1948–49. We stay on in the big house with our nanny, Miss Prior.

When Mother and Father finally do come back to Port

My sister sends a photo of herself to our parents.
She writes, "I hope you have a nice time on the boat.
The garden is looking nice. Love from Maxine."

❦

Elizabeth, the town where Father was born, he has a heart attack.

As if in sympathy I, too, fall ill with scarlet fever and lie flat on my back in the green-walled nursery with its big bay window that looks over the lawn, where I have seen the tick birds, big white birds, pecking in the grass at dawn.

My sister and my cousin and aunt leave me to go down to the sea to be with my mother and father, but I have to remain lying flat in the half dark, the curtains drawn on the bright light, fed slimy tapioca, which feels like tadpoles swimming down my throat, sucked through the spout of a teapot. The skin peels off my pink hands and feet from the high fever, this in the days before penicillin. I am tended by strangers brought in, I presume, because of the seriousness of my illness. A day and a night nurse are at my side to take care of me with my nanny, who comes in for an hour between their shifts, a moment when I choose to bestow upon her, the only familiar face and hands, the gift of my excrement in the chamber pot.

The night nurse sits by my bed in the blue light, her white uniform straining over her curves, crunching on Cadbury's chocolate biscuits, all through the long lonely nights. I wait for Mother to call, which she does every morning faithfully, only her brief bright voice connecting me to something familiar, as I lie there, unable even to sit up.

———————————— ❧ ————————————

Eventually, I am taken down to join Mother and my sister in Port Elizabeth on the Blue Train by the nanny. We visit my father in the hospital. He lies in his bed and makes fun of the nuns who care for him.

Later, Mother brings Father back to Johannesburg on the Blue Train to lie in a darkened room with an oxygen cylinder glinting silver by his bed.

My sister and I are together in the green nursery on the other side of the house, when our mother comes in without her makeup in her maroon dressing gown, one morning early. She leans langorously against the lintel and looks at us blankly before she announces the news, which my sister has already told me.

Maxine had run into our parents' bedroom, which was at the end of the corridor. A nurse in a white cap thrust her rudely out of the room, but not before Maxine saw our father lying gray and still, she could see, dead on the bed. "I'm sure Daddy's dead," she told me, running back into the nursery.

Later, I am not quite sure if my sister told me this, or I was the one who glimpsed this myself. I see my father lying gray on the bed. Have I imagined this or seen it through my sister's eyes?

Now Mother says, in a voice that sounds harsh and angry

---

to us, that our father has died. It is the same voice that I will hear when she announces the death of my sister.

I am eight years old and my sister, ten, at the moment of our father's death. Mother does not gather us up into her arms or comfort us, in my memory, but turns from us, her face pale and strange without her makeup, altered, masked.

We are all as altered, as I will be on discovering my child's deafness. I stand before the mirror on the back of the cupboard door and look at my own face, my thick blond plaits with the butterfly bows, the gash of my mouth. It behooves me to cry for my father, this man I hardly know. My sister, who knows all, tells me I do not have to cry, so I do not.

We are not taken to the funeral but play in the rock garden among the nasturtiums and the white daisies in the everlasting sunshine. The sun is what remains constant in these memories. I remember bright red shiny shoes, a new yellow dress made of organdy, garish orange nasturtiums, an aunt who is particularly kind. Our father has disappeared, almost as though he never existed.

We will never get to see him again. We are not taken to see our father, to say a last farewell, the way I will go to my sister to see her body in the morgue. Nor does anyone talk about his death or even say much about his life. It is part of the silence around us.

My sister's reported last and secret glimpse of my dead father, when she was thrust out of the room as though she had seen something shameful—a primal scene, love and death—will be the last time we see him. His death and his life are both muffled in mystery, Mother's mystery. For us it is almost as if he exists only in some mythic realm in our mother's mind.

XV

BABIES

THE BABIES KEEP COMING, BEAUTIFUL BABIES, WHO WILL somehow survive all the tragedies up ahead. More babies are born in foreign places. Maxine's third child, a little girl, arrives in London, as Carl is now studying cardiothoracic surgery in Edinburgh, and they decide London will be easier for the family during the week. On weekends my sister joins Carl in a rented house in Scotland.

Mother invites us to stay at Brown's Hotel to be with them. In the city Maxine has rented a narrow house with steep stairs and windows that look out on a leafy London square, Brompton Square. It is there that Simone is born, sweet Simone, another blond baby, who will turn into a loving child who sings and dances like her mother, and who will inherit my sister's smile.

The four children in Brompton Square:
Lisa, Sasha, Vaughan, and Cybele.

Michael and I arrive shortly after the birth with our two girls, Sasha and Cybele, and climb the stairs to help bathe the skinny pink baby in the sole bathroom at the top of the house. Mother takes us all to the ballet and to have tea at Brown's.

Ines, the Italian cook from Rapallo, comes to help and make her delicious beef stew with artichokes. She takes the eldest boy out one day to Hyde Park, where she manages to lose him for a while.

My sister visits Carl on the weekends. We will all follow him there. It is cold, and it rains all the time, and we can see nothing of the Lake Country.

We visit Edinburgh Castle and hear about Rizzio's murder by Mary Stuart's jealous husband, Lord Darnley, and we are shown the bloodstains on the floor.

XVI

ESCAPE

WE LEAVE OUR HUSBANDS AND EVEN THE CHILDREN WHO ARE born by then (six of them at this point, if I remember rightly) without too many qualms. We are in search of the art I am now studying at the École du Louvre.

We are happy to look at life on our own, to see the world as we did our garden as children, through the prism of our own imaginations or those of the artists we admire. We are eager to grasp at least an ephemeral illusion of freedom. We are happy to be together. The memory of these lost moments comes back to me now with all the ache of their vivid detail.

Mother lends us her Spanish driver, Luis, and his car, which he has had painted gold. He is a terrible driver and passes only if there is another car coming dangerously toward him in the other lane, but we set off joyfully, going through the lovely, leafy tree-lined roads of the Île-de-France. I see us at Chartres, standing together and lifting our gazes high to admire the blue stained-glass windows. We go on to the Romanesque churches at Autun and Vézelay. We visit the châteaux of the Loire: Chenonceau, Azay-le-Rideau, Blois.

We wander around Chenonceau and learn of the intrigue in the lives of the queens and kings: Henri II, who took the castle for his mistress, Diane de Poitiers, whose initials are everywhere, and Catherine de Medici, who was Henri II's wife, and who reclaims the castle as soon as the king dies. We learn of the White Queen, the wife of Henri III, the king who was murdered, and how she wore white after his death until her own.

When Maxine goes home, she writes that Mother has decided to allow our beloved servant, John, to leave her and go up to the big house to work for my sister.

XVII

BLACK AND WHITE

JOHN IS THE ONLY SERVANT WHO COMES WITH US TO THE boardinghouse in Parktown, where we go after my father dies at sixty-one. Maxine is ten and I am eight. Even the white nanny, a Miss Prior, hired by our father from an advertisement in *The Lady*, leaves, clacking the door behind her and firing her parting shot, saying, "These children would be better off in an orphanage."

John is the only one who remains. He is a tall, very darkskinned, distinguished Zulu servant, who stood straight and perfectly still, his face expressionless, while our parents ate in the big dining room with its French doors that opened onto the lawn at Crossways.

He is the one who brought a birthday cake to me at Crossways, when I had scarlet fever and had to lie flat on my back.

It was John who slipped into the darkened room secretly and wished me a happy birthday. He held the dazzling white-iced cake high in the air, all the candles ablaze, and allowed me to blow them out, though as a result of this illicit moment of joy, no one else would be allowed to eat the cake, fearing contagion, and John would be severely reprimanded.

"But it is Miss Skatie's birthday!" he insisted. He called me Skatie because of my initials, SK, which he polished on my christening cups, my silver mug, and spoon.

When we move into the boardinghouse in Parktown, Mother, my older sister, and I all sleep in one big bed, and eat in a common dining room, as if my mother wishes to hold what she has left close to her heart. My father has bequeathed most of his money to my mother, with a small part of it set up judiciously in trust for his little girls.

It is 1949, a year after the Nationalist government under Malan comes to power in South Africa and begins to put into place the absurd laws of apartheid that officially segregate the country. Not that anyone mentions this to me or my sister.

In a desperate and mad attempt to keep the different races apart—though our lives are all intricately intertwined—to negate our common humanity, a plethora of categories have been established. The different groups are given their own living spaces, their own means of transport, their own beaches, their own bathrooms, and the necessary passes to be carried in case of going from one area to the next. For the truth is, the blacks are necessary to the whites. They are the ones who do the hard, manual labor that the whites will not do. The categories are necessary in order to deny the blacks the right to enter the professions reserved for whites, and the injustice of all of this is clear to me, even at eight years old.

At the top of the pyramid there are the whites (who are distinguished in case of doubt by the pencil test: a pencil is placed in the hair, and if it falls freely, the person is classified as white) and at the very bottom there are the blacks or Bantu, which include all the different tribes, like the Xhosas, the Shona, the Zulu.

Then there are the "coloreds," those of mixed blood, many of them living in the Cape, some of whom were once on the voters' rolls but have since been denied the right. They often speak Afrikaans (having obviously white Afrikaans-speaking ancestors, though no one mentions this!) and are generally considered slightly better than the blacks because of their white blood.

There are the Indians, many of whom were brought out to South Africa to work in the sugarcane fields and are also segregated second- or third-class citizens, obliged to travel on the trains in third-class, for example. (The great Gandhi had been among these.) There are the Asians: the Malays and the Chinese, who are distinguished from the Japanese, who are considered almost white because of trade with Japan.

Anyone who is not white is officially segregated and given a "homeland," or anyway housed in a different area, always the less desirable areas, the less fertile agricultural land, the areas outside the big prosperous cities, areas that are without any important natural resources (gold, diamonds, asbestos, etc., in this mineral-rich country, though the blacks are brought in to mine these riches but not to profit from their sale).

Here the black people are forced to live apart from whites, often in abject penury or completely dependent for work on white-owned farms or as domestics like John in white households. The hated system of passes was instituted. This makes all blacks or what are called "nonwhite" people carry passes in "white areas" at all times—as though they do not belong in their own country—or risk arrest.

To us no one says much about this: silence, secrecy, and mystery surround us.

XVIII

A STORY

On a summer visit to Paris, when my husband and I have moved back there for his work with Pan American Airways, my sister tells me a story.

We sit side by side in the shade of the chestnut trees, their heavy leaves hanging down like ripe fruit ready to pluck. We are on a bench in a small Parisian square in the sixteenth arrondissement near our apartment on Rue de la Faisanderie. We sit in the Square Lamartine, watching our children play companionably in the sandpit.

My children already love their cousins, and Sasha, my eldest, has asked me why we don't live out in South Africa near them. Why don't we live in a big sunny house with a swimming pool like they do? she wants to know. She also

---

asks why all the white people in Johannesburg drive in cars, and the blacks have to walk at the side of the road.

She puts her little hands up against the glass, as I will do at the morgue, and she weeps at the airport, when we have to leave her cousins. My sister now has her beautiful blond boy and two adorable girls: Lisa and Simone. I, too, have a new baby girl, my third child, whom we have named Brett, from Brett Ashley in *The Sun Also Rises*, who lies sleeping beside me in her big English pram.

I see all six children grouped together like a chorus of Fra Angelico angels with the white Parisian light behind their blond heads like halos, their round smooth faces up-lifted, their blue eyes dreaming, their skin pink and white, their plum dark mouths slightly open as if in song.

My sister watches them, her skin now dusted with fine freckles, her soft curls paler, almost ashen. She says a terrible thing has happened to a friend. I notice the tears shimmering in her violet eyes and think how kind she has always been, how sympathetic to the troubles of others. Like my mother she is always a sucker for a sob story. She will literally give you the shirt off her back. I smile at her and hold her hand.

"What happened to her?" I ask.

A young wife, married to an up-and-coming doctor, had given a big party for her husband's birthday, inviting all his family and friends to attend. She cooked for days. The wife cooked a half chicken for each of the guests, served in an individual basket with a checked napkin. All the *tannies* and *oompies* and *kinders* arrived from the country to stay in the big house.

In the midst of the festivities, children splashing in the pool, people drinking beer, the sun shining brightly, laughter and shouts in the air, she looked around for her blond, handsome husband in his safari suit but could not find him.

She went through all the rooms of the big house and even down to the bottom of the garden to call him, but there was no response. Finally she went back into the house, where she found him lying on the gold carpet in his study with another young man, a doctor, their limbs entwined amorously.

"It was such a terrible shock," my sister says, putting her hands to her heart. "What do you think she should have done?" she asks me so earnestly.

"Kicked them in the balls; thrown them out of the house; alerted the authorities," I say, echoing what will be the advice my mother will give me, when I am in a similar situation.

"Oh, she couldn't do that! It wouldn't have been possible. They would have both been struck off the doctor's rolls, their careers ruined. There was their reputation to think of."

"What did she do?" I ask.

"All she could think to do was to call his father into the room," my sister says, tears spilling unheeded down her pink

XIX

JOHN

Now that we eat in the dining room of the boarding-house in Parktown with the other guests, John no longer serves us.

He lives in a small, smoky room without a window at the back of the building, and we see him less. When we do, he looks sad, his dark shiny skin has turned gray, his shoulders stooped. He has lost the prestige of his position in a grand house and garden, his status as a house servant in a large household, the respect of the maids and eight "garden boys," whom he had been able to boss around. He has become an ordinary "flat boy," who has to wear khaki shorts and shirt, sandshoes, long socks, his knees exposed.

Though Mother will move on again and again—she seems to feel better when she is moving, and John will come with us—and though she will acquire larger premises, she will never again bother with a big house and garden or a household of servants, and John's prestige, such as it was, will be lost forever, as is our illusion, after the death of our father, that white men last. Our experience with white men has been that they are mostly absent and die young.

John still walks us to the school bus in the early mornings, carrying our satchels like assegais, and looking out for what he calls *skelms* or anyone who might harm us. He still polishes the furniture, the silver, the parquet floors; he polishes our shoes to a high shine, he polishes the very soles of our shoes. He takes care of Mother.

After our father's early death, we are completely reduced to a house of women, the doors open, even in the bathroom, where we have little or no privacy. We talk to one another during our most private moments. Solitude is not something we know. We cling to what we have left. I tell Mother fiercely at eight that if she ever marries again, I will run away.

Our mother does not marry again, though perhaps not because of anything I say. She will not replace our father in her life. Often, when pressed to remarry, she says, "What would I want with some old boy?"

Perhaps she prefers her independence, the control of her large fortune, her own family. She is wary of fortune hunters and turns down an English lord who courts her. With her obliging family clustered around her she has enough company, or she thinks she does. She can do as she wishes. She keeps her troops in line. "I think I'm going to have to change my will," she says, looking at her family with a worried air, while they all scurry about to find her ashtray, her telephone book, her whiskey.

She drifts around our various dwelling places, smoking her filtered cigarettes, leaving the stain of her lipstick on their burned-out ends and on crystal glasses from which she drains her whiskey greedily to the last drop, tipping back her head.

She is often half naked, wearing her tight corsets, with the whalebones and lace and the suspenders dangling, her flesh overflowing above and below. Sometimes she wears nothing at all, with no shame, apparently, though her body, which has been large and then reduced by dieting, hangs in loose folds about her small frame. It is not a body we want to see naked.

Yet we do see it, living in such proximity. We watch in the mornings as she puts on her "foundation garment." Sweating, she tugs and pulls and wrenches the corset up over her hips and stomach; she drags it up over her damp white flesh, only to pull it down and settle it back over her hips. In the afternoon when she lies down for her rest, the corset has to be dragged off and pulled down her legs and draped over the back of a chair.

Mother does not seem to consider that her body might arouse desire even in John, who has been with us now for so many years. She does not seem to *see* him. He, too, does not look up, bent as he is on his polishing. It is as though Mother does not consider this tall, distinguished Zulu really a man, a man with desires, needs, and rights of his own. What is he to her? A child? Half a person? An animal? A eunuch? A saint? A human polisher?

Yet she is generous and concerned about his life. She takes care of him if he is ill or makes sure he has the necessary *muti*, as she calls medicine, using his Zulu word. She drives with him to the police office, sashaying in in her pearls and silk dress, to make sure his pass is in order; she pays him what are considered generous wages, gives him a "Christmas box" at Christmas, and above all, she talks to him, telling him of all the small and large events of our daily life. She tells him of our successes at school, and she listens to him with sympathy, when he confides that his own daughter, who has acquired an education, makes him eat in the kitchen when he visits her. John is an important part of her life.

She drinks more than ever now without my father's restraining presence, and in the evenings sometimes we find her slumped over, food trickled down the front of her frock or a cigarette burning dangerously low between her fingers. We call John to carry her to bed.

When the hairdresser has to cut off all my long thick hair because of the ringworm on my scalp, he lifts me up to see myself in the mirror. I burst into tears at this awful visitation from another world and dive to the bottom of my bed, refusing to come out. I lie there in the darkness, half suffocated, sobbing like Sartre, who, bereft of his curls, discovered his ugliness in this way.

"Come out, Skatie," John implores. "Too ugly, too ugly!" I exclaim, and there is nothing anyone can say to make me come out, though of course eventually I do come out for air and one of John's roasted potatoes.

He is always there, day after day after day, for better and for worse.

Once, a slim nubile thing by now, eleven or twelve, I bump into him in the narrow corridor. I am carelessly running naked, and when he sees me, he lifts his gaze with horror to the ceiling. I can still see his eyes turned back to show only the whites in an effort not to see.

When I step out of my bed one morning and accidentally put my foot on my beloved little budgerigar, a brightly colored bird I have taught to say, "Hallo! Hallo!" in a high falsetto, it is John who comes and takes the fluttering, wounded bird in his hands and swiftly wrings its neck. "Better like that," he says.

Sometimes he does disappear to see his own family, going

away for months. "Heaven knows when he'll come back. They have no idea of time, you know," Mother says. But he does always come back to us.

He is the one who loves us most and would gladly give his life for us, we believe, though we cannot speak his language, and he cannot speak much of ours. When Mother opens a malodorous cupboard and says, "John, clean it up, it smells Zulu," he will bend down wordlessly from his great height and clean.

XX

BLACK-AND-BLUE

MY HUSBAND AND I AND THE CHILDREN ALL FLY OUT FROM Paris to Johannesburg during the Christmas holidays to visit my sister and my mother. My sister comes to pick us up at the airport wearing her dark glasses. As she drives, she puts her hand to her eyes to wipe away the tears from time to time.

"Something wrong with your eyes?" I ask.

"Hay fever. Something in the air," she says, smiling, when I inquire, and indeed I remember she has suffered from hay fever as a girl at school. I can see her walking under the wisteria-covered pergola at St. Andrew's in her dark glasses, her eyes running.

Alone with Mother and my aunt in her pretty cottage in my sister's big garden with the bay window, where the pink roses used to grow outside, we sip tea.

Mother sits in her chintz-covered chair and tells us my sister is always taking refuge with her here. She runs down through the garden, escaping her husband in the main house to come to Mother.

"Black-and-blue! Black-and-blue! He beats her black-and-blue!" Mother says angrily, making a fist.

"Surely not! A surgeon, a doctor who has taken the Hippocratic oath! Do no harm! It's impossible," I say.

Mother says, "I'm afraid he is going to kill her. He'll shut her in the sauna and lock the door from the outside, or he'll take her out sailing and drown her. They have already been out and had the mast break in the wind. She was almost killed. No one told me, of course, but I read about it in the paper."

"For goodness' sake, don't exaggerate," I say.

I think, though, of something I once heard, that butchers, because they spend their time cutting up meat, were once given clemency in the case of a crime. What happens to someone who cuts into the heart and cracks the bones of the chest, day after day?

She tells me my brother-in-law has even risen one night in the dark and gone out and uprooted all the roses that used to grow around her cottage in their garden.

"The roses! I can't believe it! Why would he do such a thing?" I ask, looking out through the window.

"He replaced them with cabbages. Much more useful, he said," and she gestures toward the garden.

"I suppose he has a point there," I say.

He even wrote a letter to her, my mother says, a long letter in red ink on pink toilet paper with all his grievances spelled out.

"How can a man, a doctor, who must write his prescriptions in Latin, send his mother-in-law a letter on toilet paper?" I say. Surely she must be dramatizing? Could this be true?

Yet I should know by now that Mother does not always exaggerate: sometimes she withholds the essential truth in her stories.

XXI

MOTHER'S SECRETS

TRUTH IS IMPORTANT TO ME, AND IT WILL BE ALL MY LIFE. I will learn the value of emotional truth in fiction as well as in an essay. It is something I learn, ironically, from my mother, who tells us at a young age that without truth we cannot trust anyone. "How can I trust you if you lie to me?" she asks.

Besides, I have already noticed that it is the truth that is interesting. When Mother makes us sit through long dull dinners with her friends and family in Johannesburg, I am aware that no one is telling the truth. None of these people want to confront the truth. It is a hard thing to do. They prefer to mouth banalities, things others have said before, familiar phrases, what an editor will later call "received text," phrases that sound pleasant to the ear, sentiments that will serve to ingratiate them in my mother's heart, they hope, ultimately boring things, I think. "What a lovely dress!" "How well you look!" "You get younger and younger!" "You have lost weight!" they tell Mother, all said with a glint in the eye that tells me it is not what they think.

Yet I wonder how truthful Mother herself is. She is a woman of many secrets, many contradictory truths, I know. She maintains her eleven years with our father were the happiest in her life, but did she marry him, I continue to wonder, a wealthy man twenty years older than her, for love or for money?

Depending on the company, our mother will say our father was a brilliant poor boy who started from scratch, who walked to school across the veld without shoes, who loaded the timber onto the lorries by hand. Or she may say, on the contrary, that he was a brilliant rich boy whose family owned polo ponies and who attended the best schools, but contracted rheumatic fever and had to leave before completing his matriculation. He left his wealthy family in Port Elizabeth to come up to the Highveld and start a branch of the family timber company on his own in Johannesburg. Which version is true?

Father's family, Maxine and I do know, came out to South Africa from a small town in southern Germany, Kempten, which I will visit one day as an adult and find the graves of the Kohler family in the Protestant graveyard. I will have the strange sensation, walking through the streets of the town, that I look like the rest of the inhabitants, as though I have found my blond cousins, my uncles and aunts, my relatives among these hardy inhabitants of Bavaria, many of whom, I know, from this area around Munich, became notable Nazis.

Mother tells us Father's first wife died, which is something I will find out much later is both true and not true. Much later she explains that our father's first wife had died, yet it was not *before*, but *after* Mother met my father. She, our mother, was "the other woman." Father divorced his first wife to marry this slender dark-haired beauty with her tiny hands and feet, who would ultimately inherit his fortune in place of the first wife or her family. The first wife had a son, Maxwell, from a previous marriage, who would get nothing.

What was Mother's position in my father's household initially? How did she first come to Crossways, the big house bought for a song from a mining magnate down on his luck? Had she been a housekeeper, a confidante, a friend, a practical nurse for the ailing first wife? Had she betrayed her friend, who died six months after my mother married my father? She would tell us it was difficult to take over the household from the wife who had died.

I will discover that the three of them—my father, my mother, and the first wife—actually lived at Crossways together. They would remain in the big house after Mother

*My father with my mother and an unknown woman
at Place Vendôme. My mother is the one
holding the white handkerchief.*

married my father. For six months they lived together with the ailing first wife, until her death. Or was she ailing? What did she die of? How did she die? Was she, too, a drinker, which one of my aunts once hinted at, telling me that my mother learned to drink from the first wife? Was my mother brought in to watch over the alcoholic wife, a scenario I would imagine in my novel *Love Child*?

Did my poor father have one alcoholic wife on his hands and replace her with another? Was this the fate of so many of these colonial women, who had nothing else to do? Was this the result of the empty lives of these women, surrounded by black servants, who did their bidding? Was this the pernicious effect on all in an unjust system of caste and sex?

In the boardinghouse in Parktown without her husband or any white man permanently in the house Mother does not seem to consider herself a sexual being. She will even take me, a big girl now—eight, or is it possible, nine or ten?—into her bed and have me suck on her slack breasts.

"Look at my baby," I remember her saying to my Aunt Hazel one afternoon, when Hazel walked into the dim light of Mother's bedroom, the thick green curtains drawn on the bright light. "Some baby!" my aunt said, looking askance at me, which made me suddenly aware there was something wrong.

Once, Mother told us mysteriously, "You only fall in love once in your life."

She summons her daughters into the dining room one day, when we are twelve and fourteen. We have moved into a garden apartment with two floors and several bedrooms by then. She has something to tell us, she says, in an unusually solemn tone. She is afraid someone else might tell us, so she wants to do it first.

We sit at the round dining room table with its cream crocheted tablecloth and the fruit in the silver dish in the center. She lowers her hazel gaze to the fruit flies, hovering over the bowl on the dining room table, folds her hands, and says she was married before she married our father.

We gape and ask whom she was married to, and why she has never told us this before.

She had eloped with a Jewish man at seventeen, she says. He was a fellow diamond evaluator at De Beers with her father. They had escaped one night and driven down to Kimberley from Johannesburg, going to the diamond town in the Cape, her parents in hot pursuit.

"You mean you jumped out the window and just eloped?" we ask with awe and excitement, seeing our mother anew in this romantic, rebellious role.

She nods her head. The irate parents arrived almost immediately after her marriage, and the marriage was annulled. This is about all the information we can get out of her that day. She seems oddly ashamed and secretive about the whole event, which thrills us. We find it exciting and love the idea of the young Jewish man, an intellectual, we suppose. In our vivid imaginations he immediately becomes a philosopher, a rebel, perhaps, or a musician. We see him with a violin. This fantasy will remain in my mind, and will one day bring forth fruit.

Many years later, I will learn that she spent nine months in Kimberley, the site of the Big Hole, the largest hand-dug excavation in the world. It was here that many of the most fabulous diamonds were found, including the Hope, the Star of Africa, and the first, the Eureka. Mother stayed with her three maiden aunts in their shotgun house with a fig tree out the back, a dark narrow place. Most probably there was a child born there, a love child, given up for adoption, though Mother never mentioned this to us.

Once as children we were taken to visit our great-aunts in Kimberley. I remember how the three maiden aunts, who seemed so ancient to us, crowded around me and my sister. They fluttered and cooed and pecked at us, as though they were three birds, kept in the cage of the dark narrow hallway of their old house with the umbrella stand in the shape of a tree.

XXII

HOUSES

Maxine and I both move to beautiful new places frequently. In Paris Michael and I go from the rented apartment on Rue de la Faisanderie with its spiral staircase and marble floor to a new town house that I buy on a quiet street called Rue de Pomereu, also in the sixteenth arrondissement. We hire a decorator, a Mademoiselle Comblemal, to furnish the house with Louis XV furniture and deck chairs for its glass-floored terrace, which looks over a back garden. I buy a stone mill outside Paris in a place called Pithiviers for the weekends, where the river runs under the house.

My sister buys land in Johannesburg and has a new house built with the money my father has left her at his death.

It is a modern place, designed by a well-known South African architect, who, like my daughter Cybele, is deaf. My sister laughs and says that the man built what he wanted to build rather than what they had asked for. There are so many long slippery corridors, glass windows, inner patios, with bitter aloes and various kinds of cacti and high red-brick walls.

In the hall there is a portrait of my sister in a blue-flowered dress, as well as many paintings by the South African painter Pierneef, lovely, lonely landscapes of the South African countryside, with its dust roads, pale blue skies, and wattle trees.

The garden is landscaped by the architect's sister, with sloping lawns, an oak tree, and a fountain running over a wall into a pool.

My mother finds the modern red-brick house ugly and calls it the "Zimbabwe ruins," referring to the famous ancient ruins found in what was once Rhodesia.

There is a sauna near the pool, where I tell stories to the children when we visit. On the beach I have become the storyteller to little groups of children, telling stories and watching their faces, just as I would tell them in the dormitory at night at school.

Here, the children all lie on the cooler bottom bunks, while my sister and I swelter on the hot top ones. In the half dark and the heat I tell them stories about the Tokolosh and slip my hand down between the slats and wiggle my fingers to frighten them. They scream with fear and delight.

My sister reports that her children seem to be accident-prone and slip often on the polished floors or fall off stone walls. They are often falling, falling off walls, out of trees, banging their heads. Sometimes they have high fevers and even become unconscious. Later her older children will tell me their father beats them sometimes to the point of unconsciousness.

Maxine and I write to one another from our different distant places, and we call long-distance, but we are both taken up by our own big families, our duties as wives and mothers, our studies. We are separated by time, great distances, but above all by our own serious and often secret preoccupations.

I struggle to teach my deaf child to speak.

Every day I sit my screaming daughter in her high chair and give her lessons. She does not want to be confined, to be instructed, to practice anything. She wants to play in the sand with her bucket and spade. It is a battle of wills. While she kicks her little red lace-up shoes against the steel tray and waves her fists in the air and wails loudly at me, I hold up the animals from a puzzle. "The pig goes oink, oink. The duck goes quack, quack. The lamb goes baaah," I bleat at her, opening wide my mouth, while she opens hers to yell back at me.

Diligence, perseverance, fortitude, and forgiveness, we have been taught in boarding school, are the virtues to be prized.

XXIII

SCHOOL

A T ten and twelve we go as boarders to an Anglican boarding school for girls, St. Andrew's, established by two Scottish spinsters.

It is the first time I am separated from my sister, as she is in the senior school, and I am still in the junior. We have always slept in one room, whispering together, unheard in the night. "Do you think Mummy's mad? She is so strange at times, isn't she?" I have asked her.

"Just lonely, perhaps," she says.

I miss my sister in the long, lonely nights. We are put to bed before seven in the junior school, when the sky is still light. I wait for Saturday mornings, as I had once waited for Mother's telephone call every morning, while lying in the nursery with the scarlet fever.

It is Saturdays when my sister is allowed to walk up the hill, to cross the green lawns, coming through the shade of the wide-spreading oak trees and tall eucalyptus to visit me. She arrives once a week to help me wash my hair and then brush and comb it. Afterward, we sit out on the lawn beside the beds of bright orange cannas in the sunshine, drying my hair and listening to the voice of Elvis Presley on the gramophone. It is the Fifties.

She brushes my thick hair, now long again, until the sparks fly. I tell her I like her soft curls better than my hair, which has grown thick and straight, but it is a lie.

Here, too, as in our home, since our father has died, all the white men are dead: Sir George Farrar, a high commissioner, whose grand estate this had once been, whose portrait hangs in the headmistress's study. The gray slab of his grave and the lozenge of his dead dog's lie side by side at some distance from the white Dutch-gabled buildings with their red roofs. It is out of bounds, but we run there anyway, to lay wild irises on the gray stone and to climb up on the tombstone to lie there rigid, playing dead, something I will later describe in my novel called *Cracks*.

All our dormitories are named after dead white men, all high commissioners: Kitchener, Selborne, Athlone, and Milner.

All our teachers are women, mostly spinsters, and some

quite mad, like our choirmistress, who walks up the aisle of the chapel, swaying and sighing, her rubber-soled shoes squelching, her long white fingers clasped, her pale face rapt with religious fervor. She teaches us how to breathe from our diaphragms, how to lift our voices to the Lord. "Sing for God!" she exhorts us, as an editor will later tell me, "Write for God!"

Another will have us copy out the whole of Eliot's *The Waste Land*. "April is the cruelest month," we will obediently write, though for us in the southern hemisphere it does not make any sense. It is October, our spring, the month of my sister's death, that breeds the dead, I will discover.

Some of our teachers tell us that in the past they have associated with illustrious men. Madame C, who teaches French, says she is actually a princess, as she was married to a Roman prince from the ancient family of the C's. We are not sure what happened to her absent prince (dead, divorced, or imaginary?), or why she is now reduced to teaching French (which I afterward discover she does not know very well, all the verbs in the infinitive) out in an isolated school in the middle of the veld. Nor do we know why she was tortured during the war, though we shudder at the thrill of the thought of it. Her nails were pulled out and her body, which looks so plump, smooth, and healthy, was apparently plunged into boiling and then freezing water. (Would she not be dead? we wonder.) "The women were much braver than the men," she says stoutly, though she admits she would have told her torturers anything, if she had known anything to tell them.

She tells us to shut the windows in the classroom, so that they cannot hear our conversation in the staff room, and she makes us tell her when we have our periods. Mother is always contributing to her "charities," and consequently Madame gives me very good marks in French that I am aware I do not deserve. Later Mother will send me to spend a summer with this woman at her "finishing school" in Florence, where my sister will be waiting for me.

There is Mrs. Walker, with her white hair, who teaches us Latin and English. She will be the first person to commend me on my essays, to encourage my desire to write. She goes around the classroom asking us what we want to be when we are older. When I say "a journalist," hoping this might be a way to write, she looks very disapproving and says journalists write poor English.

She says the Irish poet, Yeats, was once in love with her. We imagine her in her youth, with her big blue eyes and smooth white skin. Did Yeats write his beautiful lines for her? we wonder. "And thereupon my heart is driven wild: She stands before me as a living child."

The only man who is always with us here, day and night, is the dead, sacrificed Jesus, whom we see daily in the chapel

in the mural with the wavy blue sea painted in the alcove behind the altar. Here Jesus walks across the water going toward
the disciples Andrew and Peter, his arms outstretched, like
Adam's toward God on the ceiling we will see years later in
the Vatican. He reaches out lovingly to his disciples.

Or we see Jesus on the wooden cross with the crown of
thorns on his head, his naked body, his arms, his feet stretched
out in pain. He is the only man whose presence is evoked
daily, the man of sorrows, who died so young for our sins.

We attend chapel every morning and say our prayers and
sing hymns to Jesus: "Morning has broken like the first
morning," we sing, and again every evening we lift our
voices to God: "Abide with me, fast falls the eventide." I
learn to play on the piano with some difficulty, practicing
again and again, in the small practice room, entering and
bowing to an imaginary audience, pretending to be at a concert, making a mistake, and then beginning again.

My sister, who is more musical than I am and plays the
piano well, plays the hymns in chapel, and we both sing in
the choir. We arrange the silver bowls of flowers on the altar, genuflect before the cross, murmur our old childhood
prayers: *Matthew, Mark, Luke, and John.*

In the dormitories, used as we both are to a house filled
with only women, naked and unashamed of her bare adolescent body, my sister drifts around dreamily, a friend will tell

me. I take off my clothes and dance the Dance of the Seven Veils, pretending to be Salome, dancing for the head of John the Baptist before the mirror.

We are a group of girls with our own unspoken rules. We are loyal above all to the group, to one another. We share our secrets. We always own up, even if it means being punished, if we are questioned by a teacher. We tell the truth. "I did it," someone says, putting up her hand.

We play the game of Truth at night in the dark of the dormitory. We put our hands into a pile and pull them out until someone says, "Stop!" and whoever has her hand on the bottom of the pile gets asked a question by the person who has her hand on the top. The rule is to answer truthfully. "I put a hairpin up my winkie," someone admits. Or, thrillingly and scandalously, "I let him put his finger up my winkie."

We choose "cracks," older girls whom we admire and whose approval we covet. "I'm cracked on so and so," we say. I leave a note in the plastic mug in the bathroom for Terra Merman, an older girl with dark skin that glows for me, and a shimmer in her dark eyes. *Will you be my crack?* I write on the note in her mug in the bathroom.

"Love your enemies, do good unto them that hate you. Bless them that curse you, and pray for them that despitefully use you. And unto him that smites you on the one cheek offer also the other. And he that takes away your cloak forbid not to take your coat also," we learn.

My classmates and I are confirmed at thirteen in our white dresses, clutching white prayer books to our chests. We confess our sins, and even at that moment I feel it necessary to tell the truth to the Anglican priest. I tell Father Walls, a heavy man in his black cassock, which is always sprinkled with flecks of tobacco, who comes on Sundays to hold the service in chapel, that I see no reason why I should not read books that have been banned, for they tell the truth, and then for some reason I burst into tears.

We swallow the wafer and the wine, the Savior's body and his blood, taking his flesh into our own, turning back our eyes with ecstasy. We sing, *"Lift thine eyes, lift thine eyes to the mountains, whence cometh, whence cometh my help. My help cometh, my help cometh from the Lord."*

XXIV

BLOODSUCKERS

MOTHER SAYS MY SISTER AND I HAVE BOTH MARRIED VUL-tures, bloodsuckers. Mother does not mince her words.

When the headwaiter bends forward politely in a restau-rant and asks if all is well, she will reply, "No, it is not! Service is terrible here!"

I have not initially told my own mother or even my sister what has happened to me, as I know from experience how Mother reacts. Perhaps I sense what she will say and do not want to hear it. She has never really approved of Michael, who is outspoken and often critical of her and the people around her, who live on her largesse.

One night, Michael drank an entire bottle of vodka and announced that he had something he had to tell me. We

———————————— ❦ ————————————

were in our double bed in the big yellow bedroom in the house I had bought in Pithiviers. The windows were open to the warm night, and you could hear the sound of the river running under the old mill, as it had done for hundreds of years. A nightingale sang its sweet song in a tree. In the soft light of the bedside lamp his Russian face looked raw, blotchy, unfinished, crinkling up like a child's, the slanting brown-green eyes small as slits.

He held me in his arms and quoted Baudelaire: I was his child, his sister, his friend. I was his soul, his other. He had to be frank with me, he said. He had always told me the truth. He could not lie any longer.

"What on earth is it?" I asked, appalled.

He sat up in the dim light, pulling at his remaining blond locks, and said he had fallen in love with someone else. He did not know what to do. He loved me so much. He loved us both. I held him in my arms, and together we wept at this calamity that had befallen us.

The next morning, after a sleepless night, I walked beneath the willow trees, not the weeping kind that lined the bank of the river that ran under the old mill. All I wanted, really, was to die, or so I thought.

I was strangely without anger or blame, or rather if I blamed anyone, it was myself. Had I loved this man as I should have? Had I not sinned grievously, too? What about the frog letter? What about my lack of desire for this young handsome man? What about my longing to escape into a world of fantasy?

XXV

FINISHING SCHOOL

WHEN MOTHER SENDS ME AT FIFTEEN TO FLORENCE TO JOIN my sister at Madame C's finishing school, Madame and my sister are waiting for me at the station.

My sister has already matriculated from our boarding school and has been attending Madame C's finishing school in Florence since the beginning of the year, which is 1956.

Finishing schools, I understand, are supposed to be places where foreign languages, deportment, flower arranging, and a smattering of history of art and music are taught to young girls, so that they can find wealthy husbands, who will support them in the style they are accustomed to, though, of course, these schools are not advertised as such.

My sister seems already to have learned a thing or two. She seems altered, other, removed from me, and now part of this strange new world and able to describe its beauties in Italian, as if she were singing in an opera: *Ecco! Il Duomo, Santa Maria del Fiore*—Brunelleschi's Dome, she sings out as we go by in a *carrozza*. She shows me the Ponte Vecchio, Cellini's statue, the Arno, the great dark river running through the city. She points out the passage the Medici used to go from one palace to the next in order to avoid the populace.

I gaze, stunned into silence, hardly able to answer her eager questions about Mother, our home, John.

I have never been to Italy before. Indeed, I have only once left South Africa, to travel to England by boat with my sister and my mother after Father died when I was eight years old. It rained most of the time, and I found it cold and damp, and Buckingham Palace not the fairy-tale palace I had imagined from picture books, perched with its turrets and flags on a hill.

Here, in this hot, bustling, brilliantly lit place, in the middle of our winter, I feel as if I am dreaming. After my long, solitary voyage, riding like a princess, sitting close beside my sister and facing Madame, I feel distanced from myself, a stranger in a strange place, a girl in someone else's life.

I see myself from afar as in a film or a book, as I am to do so often in my life, a voice in my head, a secret sharer, recording my own existence: a young girl in a rumpled navy linen suit, a straw hat, dark rings of fatigue beneath her slanting eyes.

On our arrival in the dark hall of the apartment with its heavy furniture and ornate round mirror on the wall, I stand there surrounded by my bags on the slippery, dark red marble floor. The ancient floor slopes and makes me feel I might slip. Perhaps because of the long airplane voyage, I am giddy, afraid of losing my footing. I feel as if I am on the swaying deck of a ship, as Madame asks me, "*Chérie*, did you bring Mother's traveler's checks with you, as she promised me?"

I have been told to tell the truth and answer a question when asked. I nod my weary head and remember how Madame C would accost our mother to tell her how lovely she looked, when she came, dressed in her pearls, her organdy dresses, leghorn hats, and kid gloves, to chapel at the school on Sundays, and how Madame would press Mother to contribute to one or the other of her "charities," which resulted in my good marks in French. Now I understand she is after the traveler's checks.

She sighs and explains, as though her protection were urgent, thieves hovering nearby, "Sign the traveler's checks over to me, will you, dearest? It would be better for me to put them away in my safe immediately." Before I can gather my wandering wits or think of a polite reason to refuse, she has had me sign and hand over the considerable number of traveler's checks I have brought with me. Then she smiles and tells me to have a quick shower and to dress fast, for we are going to a concert that very evening, which is to be held in the courtyard of the Pitti Palace, nearby.

Alone in our room, my sister protests. "Why on earth did you give her all our money?" she exclaims, but I shrug and ask what else I could have done, and she looks at me with sympathy and sighs. "You must be exhausted," she says.

My sister helps me unpack—I have brought heaps of fancy frocks, which I will not wear, before we are both called forth for the concert.

So there I sit, in the courtyard of the Pitti Palace, that first evening in Florence, listening to Vivaldi's Four Seasons (or so it seems to me) and the sound of the fountain playing, all of which comes to me in my jet-lagged state like a dream. The voyage from Johannesburg, an endless one in those days, made alone, with several stops on the African continent and Europe, makes me feel I have left myself behind with Mother and John, and that this surely is someone else, a stranger, sitting here, gazing up at the sliver of moon in the still blue sky.

Giddily, I stare up at the sky lit up by the stars and a silver moon, my heavy head falling forward onto my chest from time to time, half dead with fatigue, and then jolting back upward in awe and amazement at the strangeness of it all: the ancient walls, the musicians in black-tie, Vivaldi's Four Seasons, the elegant Italians in their jewels around me, all the beauty of the scene. I keep glancing at my sister's smooth, heart-shaped face for reassurance, but even she looks altered, other, years older than me.

Our days slip by fast in an almost continuous daze. We rise late, as adolescents do, and are left to our own devices, lounging lazily in our pajamas in the bright mornings in the rented rooms of the old palazzo. We lie around, reading our books and sipping great cups of caffe latte in our pajamas or slipping out into the street for coffee and a brioche, trying to avoid the stares and calls of the Italian men.

My sister and I share a room. The walls are white and decorated with gold filigree, a little chipped in places, the ceilings and the windows high. Many of the rooms are empty, as most of the girls have gone home during the summer months. Only one girl, Sally, remains. She is from England. Madame at this point does not have many charges on her hands to "finish."

She does not appear until lunch, when we are served great heapings of pasta or something called Florentine soup, which consists mainly of bread in broth, all of this accompanied by large glasses of wine, which Madame herself pours from vast round straw-covered vats. For some reason—I have never seen this done before or since—she mixes the red and the white together in our glasses, a toxic brew. "Drink up!" Madame exhorts us, though we are not accustomed to drinking wine at meals and certainly not at lunch. My sister and I do as we are told, my sister's cheeks flushing bright red, her violet eyes shining glazedly.

"No inhibitions!" Madame C orders us at these long, heavy luncheons, as though we could control the unconscious. "I don't want any inhibitions here!" she says imperiously, waving a plump arm around, as though inhibitions might lurk in the corners of the room or behind the curtains like goblins, ready to pounce. Perhaps Madame has read Freud or one of his disciples. In any case she maintains that repression is not good for us, and that we should speak freely and frankly of our most hidden feelings.

We gaze at one another blankly or giggle a little, half drunk on this strange mixture of wine, not knowing exactly what we are supposed to say. What is it that we are repressing?

I think of the stories Madame herself has told us at school, how she would put a finger to her lips, open her dark eyes wide, and say, "Pull down the shutters, girls, close the windows," so that none of the teachers in the staff room could hear the "lesson" she was giving.

I remember how she would ask which ones of us had our period, which she called the "curse," and tell us about the punishments meted out by the nuns in her convent school in

Brussels, where her fingers were rapped with a ruler, or she was made to kneel for hours in the corner of the room for some minor misdemeanor, or she might go on to tell us, even more thrillingly, how she had been tortured during the war. Where or why this had happened was never explained. Was this all true or just some sort of sadomasochistic fantasy? Why is she always talking about suffering, about repression, about inhibition?

Are we supposed to come up with something of this sort? Is this the sort of thing that is repressed? How could one know such a thing? We are vaguely afraid it might be something sexual, and I think of how I have let eager boys kiss me in the dark of hot, tangled gardens and felt vague longings for them. But I have also, once, let my best friend hold me in the dark of the dormitory and fondle my new breasts. What do I prefer: the hard, thrusting bodies of young boys or the soft, safe, yielding gentleness of girls?

I consider certain furtive desires in the warm nights, moments of solitary pleasure in the dark. Am I supposed to speak of this at luncheon?

"Come here, Sheila," our former French teacher calls to me one afternoon and ushers me into her shuttered study with its daybed, striped cashmere shawl, and wide Louis XVI leather-topped desk before the creeper-covered window. She tells me she often spends her sleepless nights in this room, doing her accounts or writing letters. "I hardly sleep at all," she maintains, putting her plump fingers to her brow, though as far as we can see she, never rises before noon. Then she stares at me with her piercing dark gaze and says, "I have something for you," turns her back on me, and runs her plump fingers over the books in her bookcase. What does she want to give me?

I stare at her barrel-like shape and wonder what had brought this middle-aged woman all the way out to our isolated boarding school in the middle of the veld, where I had been a boarder since I was ten years old.

Was she perhaps, like many of the foreign staff, avoiding a troubled past in that isolated place? Her main claim to fame, as far as I could gather, was that she had married a member of a princely Italian family, and therefore maintained she was a princess. Probably, though, she had no right to the title, having married the younger son, I was told by one of the other teachers.

Had she been fired from our boarding school by our headmistress, who had perhaps discovered some of her many indiscretions despite the closed windows?

And why has our mother entrusted both her daughters,

ages fifteen and seventeen, as well as our entire travel allowance for the year, to Madame's care?

Madame says, "I think you might find this book interesting," and takes a thick volume with a dark cover out of the bookcase that lines one of the walls. I thank her, wondering what dull tome she is obliging me to read, and take the volume back to my room.

I turn the pages fast with amazement, titillated, enthralled, and shocked. The book is a famous lesbian novel—surely an odd choice to give a fifteen-year-old pupil in one's charge. It is called *The Well of Loneliness* by Radclyffe Hall and was first published in 1928.

As I read, I wonder why Madame has chosen to give me this book. Is Madame a lesbian? I remember how she would go on walks with us across the veld around our boarding school, the vast property that had once belonged to Sir George Farrar. We would visit his grave, which lay at some distance from the white-gabled buildings. Madame would pant and struggle along beside us on her narrow ankles. "Just put one finger on my back, to help me up the hill, just one finger," she would tell us.

And more importantly, I think as I read, is it possible that Madame has understood that I must really be a lesbian, too?

After all, I am not sure what I do desire. Am I really in love with any of the eager, sweaty boys who have held me so fiercely in their arms and kissed me in the tangled back gardens of Johannesburg? Might I rather be in love with a girl? I seem to have remained in a childish state of polymorphous perversity.

Perhaps I find the reason for Madame's choice, while wandering around her study one morning. Up earlier than anyone else, I dare to wander into Madame's sanctum sanctorum. There I find a half-written letter lying, lit up by the early morning sun, coming in through the open window. Already the budding writer (I keep an imaginary diary all about meeting boys on the beach and swimming naked in the surf, which my mother reads and thinks is real), and, ever curious, looking for intrigue and answers to my many questions, I am irresistibly drawn to peep at the page to see who Madame could be writing to in her solitary life.

The letter is addressed in English to *My dearest, dearest beloved*. Of course, I read on with interest. Is it possible that this stout middle-aged teacher with her white hair and oily skin could have a beloved? The letter, not really to my surprise, is a passionate appeal to another woman, the mother, I will find out from her only other charge, the pretty English girl, Sally—*I long for you in my wild nights*, she writes.

After lunch, rather than taking us to see any of the famous churches or the museums with their Madonnas by Raphael

---

or Andrea del Sarto, or Michelangelo's sculpture of David, or even the countryside around Florence, the Tuscan towns, Madame takes the three of us to her elegant club, which lies in a large oak-shaded garden with blue and white agapanthus growing under the trees and a long blue pool. In our demi-inebriated state none of us protests. Instead, we sprawl sleepily in our bikinis on towels in the grass, stretched out in the sun beside the pool, whispering to one another, as we might just as easily do in South Africa.

Madame plops herself down near us in the shade in a deck chair in a striped dress, her short legs apart, her feet dangling. She keeps us entertained and enthralled with a running commentary on the young men who pass us by, pointing out the mysterious and interesting parts of their anatomies: "Look at the way he is staring at you and swelling in his bathing suit," she says, as some strapping Italian youth lingers near us, caressing us with his dark regard. Madame explains how men's parts expand like flowers in the sun in the proximity of our feminine charms. We listen, appalled and fascinated and half drunk with wine, warm air, and one another's company.

Later, Madame takes the three of us on a voyage. Madame's as well as Sally's expenses for the voyage, indeed for the entire summer, I believe, are paid for by our traveler's checks.

We are driven to Venice by car. When the chauffeur comes

to a stop, not being able to venture any farther because of the canals, Madame tells him to continue. When he says he cannot, she shouts, *"Avanti! Io sono la Principessa C!"*

The man tells her in no uncertain terms that he does not give a fig who she is, that he can go no farther, and we are obliged to get out and have a gondola convey us and our luggage to our hotel. I have a photo of us in a gondola with Madame reclining opposite us and smiling benevolently at my sister and me.

After Venice we go to the island of Giglio, which means *lily* in Italian. The place is quite wild and primitive, and we spend much of our time on the white beach. It is, surely, an odd destination for young girls who have never been to Italy and who have come to study the language and the culture. Why are we not taken to Rome or Milan or even Assisi? Perhaps the reason is Giglio, and our hotel is particularly inexpensive. Most of the day Madame leaves us to our own devices on the beach, where the local boys try to approach us.

When I return home and tell Mother what has happened to her traveler's checks, she is appalled. "The woman is a thief!" she says. I don't tell her about the book Madame has given me to read.

My sister beside Madame C with Sally and me opposite.

XXVI

ADVICE

When I finally tell Mother about my husband's love affair, her advice is, "Give him a kick in the balls! Throw his clothes out the window!" She sees things in black-and-white, and I see the gray areas.

"Oh, Mother," I say. "I love him, and he loves me."

"You don't hurt someone you love," she says.

I will also try to advise my sister.

Maxine and I sit by her pool in the sunshine and watch the children swimming and splashing about. I notice the tears shining in her eyes. I ask her what is happening. Is she in danger of any kind?

She lowers her voice and admits her husband beats her. She does not know what to do. I beg her to leave him, but she says it is impossible. "He would never let me escape. He has all the childrens' passports locked in the safe. He has me followed by a detective and makes sure I am home for meals, even for luncheon."

"See a lawyer, then," I urge.

"I can't go. He has me followed, or he follows me, and then he beats me," she says.

She asks me to go and see the lawyer for her.

I drive on my own into Johannesburg and see the man in his office myself. He says politely but firmly, "If your sister is unable to come to see me, how will she obtain a divorce? She's the one who needs it, no? Have I got this right?"

Is she the one, or is it me? Who needs the divorce? What is it about us both that shackles us to these men, who cause us such grievous harm?

XXVII

IDENTITY

WHEN I MATRICULATE FROM ST. ANDREW'S WITH A DISTINC-
tion in history, at seventeen, I decide to leave this home, filled
with women whose main occupation is to shop and knit. I will
leave this country, where white is kept so artificially separated
from black. My sister has already left home. She is at the University of Cape Town, studying languages.

It is 1959, a year before the Sharpeville Massacre, when
South African policemen fire on unarmed blacks peacefully
protesting the pass laws that restrict their movement within
white areas. Sixty-eight people are left dead on the ground.
When the policeman in charge, a Lieutenant Colonel Pien-
aar, is asked if he has any regrets, if he would have done
anything differently, he says yes, indeed, he would have had
more ammunition on hand.

If I am going to write, which I have wanted to do since I was five years old, it will be necessary, I believe at seventeen, to know who I am. Who am I?

What is it I desire?

What else am I going to write about? Or even if I were to become an actress—I sign my letters "from an undiscovered genius"—I will need to find out who I am. How does one find out such a thing?

One of the things I am most certain of at seventeen is that I do not want to be like my mother in any way. My mother, who had been a great beauty in her youth, or so she tells us, does not look like me. She is small, with dark curls and big, soft hazel eyes. She has tiny hands and feet. I am taller, with straight, thick dark-blond hair and slanting gray-green eyes. I look, if I look like anyone, more like the tall thin young man with the blond forelock and the slanting eyes who will ring our bell one evening in Rome, the man I will marry. We will often be taken for brother and sister as though we have a common ancestor, which indeed we will discover may be possible and a source of much grief. We will be told that our daughter's deafness is the result of a recessive gene that we both carry. Had either of us married someone else, this would not have happened, the doctor says.

Nor do Mother and I have the same interests, or so I

believe at seventeen. In a moment of rage I once tell her, "We have nothing in common." It seems necessary to me to escape her, in order to find out who I am. I need to flee from her excessive, permissive love, her extreme all-encompassing generosity. I need to go to some other, foreign place, or at least to find a middle zone, somewhere strange yet sufficiently familiar. I need, I feel, to escape this world of women.

I tell Mother I want to learn French.

Mother sighs nostalgically, puts her hands to her heart, and tells her younger daughter about her honeymoon at the George Cinq Hotel in Paris. My mother, who reads books by Barbara Cartland, wants me to marry an English lord. Learning French, surely, would help in this endeavor.

Mother, who speaks only English and a smattering of Afrikaans and Zulu, thinks French a considerable asset in a marriageable girl's arsenal. She thinks learning French—the most fashionable, the most elegant, the language of love—would be almost magical.

I don't tell anyone the real reason I want to leave home. Later, I will tell people that I feel my other option would have been going to jail, and I decided to take the coward's way out, though I have never engaged in any subversive political activity, never championed the rights of the blacks in any active way, and rarely read the newspaper.

What I do not tell anyone is that I want to learn French because it is *not* my mother tongue, because I have no idea who I am or even what I believe and feel it necessary to go elsewhere, to another country, a strange land where no one speaks English, to find out.

I already have some rudimentary knowledge of the French language, French history. I have heard of the French philosophers: Diderot, Voltaire, and Rousseau. I have read of the French Revolution, the Rights of Man, Robespierre and his guillotine.

Of course, I do not realize at seventeen how difficult an endeavor all of this is, and how much living, loving, suffering, and hard work is up ahead. Switzerland seems the place where I can be someone else, cloaked in the disguise, the dark mysterious folds of a foreign language with impunity, a place to find out who I really am in safety.

Switzerland, with all the cowbells, the chocolate, the cheese, the banks with their reassuring red geraniums in the window boxes, is considered ideal, a secure place for money, the very young, and the very old, a safe place for a seventeen-year-old South African girl fresh out of a girls' boarding school.

So Mother finds me a boardinghouse recommended by friends. I stay with two spinster ladies, the Mlles. Gomez, who keep a dark rooming house for young girls and make us pay extra to have a bath every night. I study French at the École Lémania in Lausanne, which is where I meet Enrico, a Roman, who is also learning French.

It is thanks to Enrico that I will spend a year in Rome, and thanks to him that I will meet my husband, Michael.

XXVIII

THE OTHER WOMAN

In Paris Michael comes and goes, dramatically, on his long legs, rushing back and forth from his family to his mistress, torn in two, guilty, a new Raskolnikov, doing one thing and immediately regretting it, getting ulcers, losing his hair, wearing a wide-brimmed hat to hide his widening bald patch, scattering the pebbles in the driveway in his green Porsche, as he drives off fast, waving his hand and calling out, "I love you! I love you!" as he goes. He is always telling me this is the last time, the last time he is leaving me, he is just going for one more weekend to tell Francine good-bye, good-bye, good-bye. Does he tell his mistress, poor Francine, the same thing?

As I walk through the streets of Paris, I seem to catch glimpses of her: she is every young blond woman who walks by me, every slim young woman seen sashaying seductively down the street from behind. I think about her almost more than him. She haunts my dreams.

Once, near the Invalides on a misty autumn day, while I'm walking with my eldest daughter, I see my husband getting out of a taxi with a slim young woman in a fur hat. For a moment I stand in the street unable to move, afraid I might fall. "Mummy, you've turned all white," my Sasha says, and I hold her hand and hurry on.

I have placed Michael's photograph, grinning, in his wide-brimmed hat, on the top of the baby grand piano I have acquired for the children's piano lessons. I sit at the window and listen to *Madama Butterfly* or *Rigoletto* or even *Don Giovanni* with the children beside me, waiting for Michael's return in the evenings. I see him striding in late, impatient, critical. "The house is in a mess," he complains, projecting his own guilt on me, no doubt. Have I no sense of order?

Yet I rush around putting flowers in the vases, making sure his shoes are shined, his shirts perfectly ironed.

Why do I act in this strange fashion?

What is wrong with me? Why am I the guilty one? Why do I seem to feel I need to prove I am a good wife?

XXIX

ENRICO

It is Enrico, the boy I meet in Switzerland, who persuades my mother to stay on for a year in Rome after the summer Olympic games.

He is a Roman aristocrat, a slight young man with a delicate face, dark, byzantine brown eyes, a straight nose, almost pencil-thin at the tip. Seventeen or eighteen years old, he is still a schoolboy, who does not even try to kiss me, yet in the light of the stars and a sliver of moon, he talks volubly in fast, accented French, as we walk through the hilly town of Lausanne. He waves his fine hands in the air. He wants to be a poet, a painter, an architect. Translating his Italian words for me, he quotes from Leopardi—*vaghe stelle dell'orsa*—from Ariosto's *Orlando Furioso*, and Dante, writers I have never read or even heard mentioned.

I will find him again in Rome when Mother and my sister, who is already studying languages at the University of Cape Town, meet me there for the summer Olympic games. It is 1960. We are staying on the Via Veneto in the Hotel Majestic, a grand place not far from the Borghese gardens.

Enrico suggests we dine, one evening, in a typical Roman restaurant. It is in the Trastevere, a dark tavernlike place where they serve Roman fare, Meo Patacca. While the waiters in white aprons, tied tightly around their waists, rush around the tables with red-and-white-checked tablecloths, holding heaped plates of pasta high above our heads, Enrico and my mother drink a whole bottle of Chianti. Someone is singing Italian songs in the background—"O Sole Mio"—while Enrico leans eagerly toward Mother, his fine face close to hers.

Mother glimmers in the dim light in her mauve knit dress, her triple string of pearls, and her multicolored diamond rings. She wears the big, rare blue diamond given to her by her father, a diamond evaluator, and said to bring bad luck. She always maintains she is a lucky woman, always wins at the races, and does not fear the superstition that surrounds the stone.

Enrico waves his fine hands in the air and repeats again and again, in his rudimentary English, "Sheila must stay Rome!" as though it is a refrain in a medieval ballad.

Mother, who is taken with Rome, the friendly people, the

hot sunny weather in July and August (our winter in the Trans-vaal), Enrico's good manners, his fine face, and his gentle nature, does as he asks.

Perhaps, too, she is not unwilling to leave South Africa for a while. It is only a few months after the Sharpeville Massacre.

Mother rents a ground-floor apartment in the elegant Parioli district, near Piazza Crati, with a high iron gate and the small front garden. It is there I will find Michael, the man who is to be my husband, standing one evening in the gloaming.

The apartment is a sprawling place. There is a large living room with blue-velvet-covered walls and sliding windows that open onto the small garden that surrounds the building. A copy of Watteau's *Pierrot* stands stiffly, his arms at his sides, his red bows on his white shoes, looking down at us blankly from one wall. There is a blue glass coffee table with bright butterflies pressed beneath the glass. There are many rooms, and we are free to invite people who might need a place to stay. Mother is always generous and responds to the suffering of others in an almost instinctive and spontaneous way. Her houses are always open to others.

She rents a bus to take us all out to Tivoli to see the fountains at night. She hires a mad maid with frizzy gray hair, who speaks some unknown dialect, and like my mother cannot cook, and she sends me eventually to the Dante Alighieri school.

My sister and I also find a private tutor who will read

Dante with us through the summer. She is recommended by the school, a dark-haired spinster (or is she a widow like our mother?) whom we call Professoressa. Everyone in Italy, we discover, has a title, or if they do not, they make one up.

The teacher has a slight stain of a mustache on her wide upper lip and lives on the other side of the Tiber River in the crowded, narrow streets of the Trastevere. She reads Dante with my sister and me, every afternoon through the summer months, her hand on her heart.

XXX

DOUBLE AGENT

"Call me anytime, darling, day or night. I understand how you feel. I've been there, too," my mother-in-law says with apparent sympathy, when I call with the news of her son's infidelity.

My mother-in-law, who now lives in a beautiful apartment in Switzerland, tells me what I want to hear, what is useful to her and her son, that it is all in my hands, that it is all up to me, up to the woman, always. He will come back to me, if I listen to her advice. She has been in the same position, she tells me, with my husband's father, and no one gave *her* any good advice. She made scenes, threw things on the floor, none of which did any good, she says. Now she is going to help me handle the situation with skill, to hold on to my man. If I care enough, if I am patient and loving enough, it is

---

possible, she tells me. She is sure of it. She gives me hope, if of a somewhat dubious kind.

I am under the impression that these calls are our secret, that I am her only source of information on the subject, but, of course, I later discover that my husband, too, is calling her during the same time, and she is listening to him and giving *him* counsel as well, which may not be what she is telling me. How can I imagine that this mother's first allegiance is not to her one and only son? How can I be so blind? Why do I not realize she is a double agent, which I later accuse her of being?

She, who has for ten years been relegated to a minor role in our marriage, is now in the center of things, like Fate, pulling the strings. She even tells me not to make love to him, which might be useful advice but is not advice I follow. I am like the character in Katherine Mansfield's wonderful story "Bliss," who, once she observes her husband's infidelity, is able to feel passion for him for the first time. It is as though Michael's passion for his mistress has ignited my own for him. Now, when it is too late, when the horse has left the stable, I desire him, as though I can feel desire only through this other woman, the mistress who is now part of him and me.

Still, here, Nonna, in a further turn of the screw, is the one in control. It is she who manipulates us. We are the "dolls" in this game—her boy and his mistress and her daughter-in-law—and we dance to her secret tune. She whispers secret advice to the one and then to the other. Perhaps only a gifted Southern lady would be capable of such delicate duplicity. How skillfully she manages us all! Or does she simply and masterfully tell me what I want to hear, and him, what he wants to hear, ultimately what is useful to her?

I do not know what she tells my husband. Does she suggest he go ahead and have some fun? Sow some wild oats? Get the girl out of his system? He married too young, and no one thought it would last this long. I know she also meets Francine and seems as fascinated with her as my husband is, as I am, or so a friend who is close to my mother-in-law will tell me. There are triangles within triangles in this complicated plot.

In my case she counsels patience. (I am, you have to understand, paying the mortgage on her apartment in Switzerland and our entire household is mainly maintained by my money.) She tells me not to make her son feel guilty: "No one wants to feel guilty, do they, dear?" she asks me.

"Indeed," I, the guilty one, say.

"Pretend he has the measles," she says. "Pretend to be asleep when he comes home late at night," she says. "The family is sacred, don't you think, darling? Do it for your girls," she says, and advises taking a lover. "It will take your mind off him," she says and laughs her coy laugh. "Goodness, here I am, his mother, telling you to do this!"

XXXI

ROME REDUX

IN THE MID-SEVENTIES, MAXINE CALLS AND ASKS ME TO MEET her in Rome, where we both spent several months, fifteen years before, and where we learned to speak an archaic Italian, reading Dante. She has something urgent she would like to discuss with me in person.

Suddenly, with her call, I grasp the opportunity for a change. I want to cease watching and standing back, submitting. I am diminished by my husband's constant infidelity. Part of my soul seems paralyzed. Now I want to drink up life again with my sister. I long to be alive, to be happy in the beautiful place where we had once been together.

So I leave my three children, who are all in school, with the eldest, now fifteen, in charge of the younger ones and the dog, and the concierge, who promises to come in to make the soup and keep an eye on things in our apartment in Paris. We have moved from the town house on the Rue de Pomereu to an apartment on the Rue Guynemer, the street that runs along the edge of the lovely Luxembourg Gardens. I leave the children money and tell the girls to walk across the gardens to McDonald's for hamburgers, which they afterward tell me they did, every day.

My sister leaves her three children—or are there four by now?—and comes to join me. Sometimes her husband forces her to have sex with him, she tells me.

My husband is off somewhere else, too. Once again, he tells me he will be gone for a few days with his mistress. He has said good-bye once again, standing in the hallway of our home, tall and loose-limbed, with his Russian cheekbones, his wide childish mouth, and the aquiline nose. He seems almost to strike up a Travolta pose, as if he might click his fingers and break into a dance in his pink shirt and elegant English tailor-made suit with the shiny gray waistcoat, his narrow English shoes. He waves his arms around and thrusts a letter into my hands.

He gives me a letter to be opened in case of emergency, with his address, and I leave for Rome.

XXXII

NEL MEZZO DEL CAMMIN

THE EARLY-AFTERNOON SUN IS WARM ON MY FACE, AS I STEP out of the airport in Rome. I am eager to see my sister again and wonder what she wants to discuss with me. I think of Carl, his impetuosity, his ruthlessness, his brutality. What has happened now?

I take a taxi into the city, staring out the window in wonder, first at the Roman countryside, the terra-cotta villas, the vineyards, and then at the city, with its wonderful pine trees with their long, long trunks and thick branches that search for light and space, opening out like dark green umbrellas.

I remember them from our stay in the Parioli, so many years before. I think of how my sister and I would take two buses in the afternoons, hanging on to the straps and swaying in our pastel-colored full-skirted frocks. I remember how up-set my sister would get, when the men called out, "*Che bam-bola!*" and tried to touch her behind. We would go across the river to read Dante with the dark-haired Professoressa in the Trastevere, just as, while children, we would cross the stile to go into the wild part of the garden.

The teacher's apartment was a walk-up on the top floor of her ancient building. Every afternoon, she welcomed us at the top of several flights of dusty red stairs, when we arrived, sweating and breathless, after our long ride, the rude shouts from the men. She stood before us in her long, dark dress, looking pleased and happy to oblige but somewhat surprised that these two young South African girls continued to come, carrying a fat envelope with cool cash in their hands, paying to read Dante for pleasure, for instruction, to learn how to live, all through the hot summer months, when everyone else was at the beach.

She opened the door of her small apartment and ushered us into the dark rooms, crowded with large well-polished ugly furniture with claws for feet.

Her elderly mother shuffled out in her slippers to serve us lemon tea and pastries dusted with icing sugar. Then we sat around the shiny mahogany dining room table, and the Pro-fessoressa read Dante with her hand on her heart.

Nel mezzo del cammin di nostra vita
mi ritrovai per una selva oscura,
ché la diritta via era smarrita.

We intoned solemnly, as we had when reciting the prayers we had learned as children.

Now, surely, we are in the middle of our lives, I think, as the driver drops me off at the Hassler, a hotel at the top of the Spanish Steps, where I have booked us a room.

As I stand at the window of our room staring at the pink and white azaleas that run over the stone steps, cascading down to the boat-shaped fountain below, after the endless *grisaille* of the Parisian winter, I feel suddenly as if someone has turned on the color in my life. Perhaps for the first time since Michael announced his affair, I think, *I'm happy to be on my own, taking in life just for me, for me.* I keep repeating, *How lovely, thanks be to God for such a lovely day, thank you for Rome!*

Since Michael has fallen in love with another woman, I find myself murmuring little prayers that spring spontaneously to my lips, coming directly from my childhood, from my Anglican boarding school, from my heart, though I am not a churchgoer at this point in my life. Sometimes I murmur, for some reason, *Please, God, forgive me!* Surely I must have committed some sin to be punished thus? What is it I have done or failed to do?

I begin to unpack. I leave the prescription from the fancy doctor I have consulted in Paris on the desk by the telephone. I will have to find a nurse to give me the daily shots.

"What's wrong with me?" I asked the doctor I consulted. Since Michael has taken a mistress, I have become prone to dizzy spells. I feel the ground is tilting slightly under my feet, as if I might fall at every step.

I remember the doctor saying something mysterious about having the sort of thing women would go to the South of France to cure. "A change of air might help," he said without much conviction.

XXXIII

DRAMA

Since John's arrival in my sister's house, he must know what is going on there, surely, as servants always do, and though he may not be called upon to help his "master," he must know what his "master" is doing to his "mistress."

He will play an important part in the drama of my sister's life and death.

Later, I will write about this in a story called "Africans." In the story it will be John, the beloved servant, who has brought the two girls up, who, in a neat reversal, holds his "mistress" down for his "master's" convenience.

At the time of that writing, though John is long since dead, will never read my words, I feel that using this trick of fiction is a betrayal of the brave man I have perhaps loved the most in all my life. In a cruel final scene this old faithful servant finally turns on his "mistress," and holds her down on the bed while the *"baas"* beats her with his belt. Here I have had the gall to use this devoted man as a character and had him act in a way that is useful and effective for the structure of the story I wanted to tell.

In reality Carl calls the black female servants into the bedroom to help the "master," and they are forced to participate in a particularly South African form of wife-beating, holding my struggling sister down on the bed, while he beats her. The role John plays, though innocent, will prove to be even more terrible in the end. But I will get to this, as Dostoyevsky says, in its proper place.

Once, only once, does John give an inkling of his feelings. We are driving in the car, and he is sitting beside me and my husband. We are on a visit to South Africa. In response to my husband's question about the position of blacks in this country, John says in his solemn way, sitting huddled as close to the car window as he can, his bony shoulders scrunched up around his ears, "The white man has failed us."

Indeed.

XXXIV

ARRIVAL

At the hotel in Rome, waiting for my sister, I take what is often the cure for whatever ails me: a hot bath. I turn on the taps and get into the steaming water. Before leaving, I had given Michael the hotel's address and telephone number. For a moment I think I hear the telephone ringing, but when I turn off the taps, I realize it is only the sound of the traffic in the busy street.

I bathe and then go downstairs to wait for my sister in the inner courtyard, with its plants and fountain, sitting there in the twilight, sipping a glass of wine, reading, I remember, a book by Simone de Beauvoir, *La Femme Rompue*, which is not improving my mood. The elation I have felt on arrival is fast disappearing, and I am worrying about my sister. Why is she so late? Could something have happened to her?

I think of the troubling story my brother-in-law told us of my sister waking one morning feeling very ill. "She lay beside me saying she thought she was dying," he said and then went on to say that he was terrified, because he imagined he would be accused of killing her.

"Why on earth would they accuse you?" I asked innocently at the time, though my words would come back to me with an ominous ring. As I write of them today, hindsight casts its dark wing and colors them. For who else but someone with murder in his heart would have that troubling thought? Was this something Carl had planned to do for a long time or at least considered? Was it a constant possibility in his mind? A way out of his unhappiness?

I think of the boardinghouse where the three of us lived for a while, all crammed into a small space, with Mother drinking too much and my sister so distressed about leaving the big house and garden, the dogs, the piano she loved to play, all of which my mother had sold or put away in storage, in a moment of panic, I presume. I remember how Mother would say to us, "You girls have no idea how hard it is to bring up two children on your own without a man." Indeed, I think how right she was. Perhaps that is what growing up means: slowly realizing how right your mother has been.

What could have happened now?

I worry, too, on my second glass of wine, about the

children on their own. Usually I am there in the afternoon in the kitchen, when they come back from school. While I cook, they do their homework.

Then she is here, appearing, it almost seems, magically, as though she has brought the African sunlight with her into the gloaming of the Roman courtyard. She stands before me, her blond curls in disarray, her face shining. For a woman of her age—she must be thirty-four or -five—she looks remarkably young, her skin still smooth, her body slim, lithe. I can see her trying to help the bellboy with all her luggage. She explains she had had to help someone who had several children find a taxi, before she got one herself.

As she speaks, I hear my own voice coming to me, and I remember how our voices have always been indistinguishable on the telephone, and how I had sometimes asked her to answer for me, if I was engrossed in a book.

"How lovely to see you. You look marvelous in a mini. You have lost weight," she tells me, which is true, though I am not sure it is a compliment. Since Michael has gone, I sleep badly and eat little. I often rise early in the mornings to go running on the outside of the railings around the Luxembourg Gardens with the dog, the earth seeming to tilt as I go around and around at dawn, staring at the white statues of queens long since dead, but I do not tell her this.

In the hotel room my sister holds me close and comments

---

again on my weight. She wants to know what is happening. She says, "He seemed so crazy about you, such a solid, responsible man!"

"I used to call him my Rock of Gibraltar," I tell her.

"Where is he now?" she wants to know, and I tell her about the letter with his address, which I have promised not to open except in an emergency.

"How cruel of him," she says, and afterward I think how perceptive we can be about other people's problems but not our own.

The next morning, I lie in bed beside my sister, as we used to do as girls in the nursery. She is still sleeping soundly, an arm over her face, the light sheet like a shroud over her soft body. I think of my children waking alone in the apartment on the Rue Guynemer and wonder if they will remember to walk Max—poor sweet Max, a beautiful chocolate-brown German Braque with such sad eyes! We have named him after my father.

I lie there, listening to the sound of the spring swallows, and watch my sister sleep, remembering the house and garden where we grew up, and how freely we roamed the land together, half naked, as children: bare-headed, barefoot, swimming in the big pool, picking armfuls of bright flowers and entwining them in our hair, around our ankles and wrists; gathering oranges and lemons, which fell at our feet; plucking warm sour tomatoes from the vine, bending over to eat them, the juice squirting into our mouths and onto the earth; climbing up into the dark, cool leaves, hiding in our safe places, the jacarandas, the lychee tree, which spread its heavy branches to the ground like a canopy at the bottom of the garden; stuffing the sweet fruit into one another's mouths.

Maxine is no longer that dreamy, quicksilver girl with the light laugh, the white curls, whom I remember. She has given up her languages, her dance. She no longer sings.

When she wakes, we lean on the sill in the early sunshine, listening to the bells tolling the hour, watching the fork-tailed swallows circling in a pale sky, swooping over red-tiled roofs. "You cannot imagine how wonderfully peaceful it feels here with you," she says. "I wish we could stay forever."

"We have to go back to our children," I say, and sigh. I tell her that I keep dreaming that the children are lost, have fallen down to the bottom of the sea, and I am swimming around breathlessly, trying to find them in the seaweed, before they drown. I am afraid I might lose them, as I did the dog once. I tell her I had forgotten Max, the dog, one afternoon, tied up

———————————— ❦ ————————————

at the baker's and howling, until the police came to claim him, and he had to be fetched from the station.

I tell her that really I do not feel at home anywhere, anymore, and certainly not in Paris, except perhaps with her, my sister. She nods, says that no one speaks the language we speak; no one finds the same jokes funny; no one laughs as we do together. No one understands.

"The language of childhood," I say. "But you can't leave the children alone. You have to go back."

She suggests we go out to a café for breakfast. "This place costs a fortune," she says. She has always been the thrifty one, has done well with her gold shares. She has a better sense of what to do with money. She has been more sensible than I have been. I have left the handling of my inheritance to Michael, as though it were his money.

We walk together down the Spanish Steps, going through the throngs of people, vendors selling absurd toys, postcards, pens, tourists milling, the bright pink and white azaleas spread out like scarves.

We sit on the edge of the Bernini fountain, and I watch her face in the early spring light. I ask her again about her husband, the children. Has she told me everything?

She says her husband is in great demand as a heart surgeon. He comes home late at night, exhausted, bad-tempered. She has to do everything for him, pay all the accounts—he buys nothing, not even a bottle of beer. It is she who must organize the servants, the house, and of course, she never does it quite well enough for him. He does such demanding work. I know the story she is telling me.

She says that a heart surgeon has to make such difficult decisions. They have to be made in a split second, questions of life or death. He tells her the fact that she can never make up her mind about anything has made him fatally indecisive. Sometimes he says he would like to give it all up and retire and grow wine in the Cape.

"He *says* he adores me, that he has put me up on a pedestal."

She says, "Of course, the patients often die—heart operations are very difficult." Her eyes fill with tears.

"Something wrong?"

Her little chin trembles, and she wipes her eyes. But she just takes my hand and shakes her head. "You have enough on your mind at the moment," she says. She hesitates to tell me about the latest shocking events in her life, about Carl's latest exploits. He seems to be a man who feels all is permitted to him, that he can follow his desires wherever they might lead.

What makes him think he is above the law in every way? Is nothing sacred to this man?

She says nothing more. How we hesitate to share our sorrows, proud and afraid of hurting one another!

Horse-drawn carriages rumble past on the cobblestones, the forked-tailed swallows swoop down low, the Roman men sidle up, dark eyes on my sister. A handsome Roman policeman in his white uniform and white helmet is directing the traffic. He lifts his baton with elegance. An April morning, Rome, the beginning and the end of things.

We have breakfast in a café and my sister now tells me how her husband has been found trying to molest a little boy, a friend of his son, in the changing room by their pool. The parents have complained. What should she do?

I pass on my mother-in-law's dubious advice. "For goodness' sake, if you feel you cannot leave Carl, at least go on with your own life. Take a lover! Take one for every day of the week. Seize the day!"

We are the blind leading the blind.

XXXV

LOVERS

MAXINE AND I WALK DOWN THE VIA CONDOTTI WITH ALL its elegant shops, going in to buy underwear and matching silk nightgowns, hers in pink and mine in white, or was it the other way around? In the end I will get both.

When Maxine leaves me in Rome to go on to Istanbul, she takes my advice, or perhaps chance just plays its part. I can only hope she has a few moments of pleasure in her life. From Istanbul she writes to me: *I saw him come walking across the tarmac looking like a cross between Donatello's and Michelangelo's David.* Who could resist?

What happens next is in its own way much worse than my fictional account in "Africans." As is so often the case, truth is much crueler than fiction. It is something that I had conveniently blocked out of my mind.

When Carl finds a letter from my sister's Turkish lover in my sister's handbag, he cuts his veins and lies bleeding on the stairs of the house.

It will be John who finds him there and calls my sister to come and help. Without this good and faithful man, my-brother-in-law would have died, and my sister would have lived. It will be John who carries the *"baas"* to the car, so that my sister can take him to the hospital, where he recovers, and then comes back home to tell the children their mother is a slut and to make remarks about her lover every time anyone mentions "Turkish delight."

I, too, will take a lover:

I receive a letter from a man whom I once had a crush on as an adolescent in South Africa. I have known him since I was fourteen. He is coming to Paris for a few nights for business.

A dark-haired rugby player with a beard, broad shoulders, and very blue eyes, he had been a brilliant boy, a star student at his boy's boarding school in Natal, captain of the rugby team and, unusual for a South African adolescent, a lover of classical music. I remember the photos of famous composers he had pasted on the back of the doors of his gramophone—two strange men: Gustav Mahler and Igor Stravinsky. He tried to share his passion with me, but at fourteen I was not able to appreciate his favorite symphonies and simply giggled.

Now I imagine going to a concert with him, and holding his hand, though I realize that he may no longer be up for classical music.

He has gone big-game hunting in what was Rhodesia and was bitten by a tsetse fly and has almost died. This has perhaps left irremediable damage to his brain. In any case he has changed, apparently. He has not fulfilled his early promise and has remained in the bush, as though he cannot move forward in his life. He has become a Big White Hunter, taking people out on safaris to shoot game. Now he writes to say he is briefly coming to Paris for business.

I pack the entire family off to the house in the country, that Friday afternoon. I tell my startled husband I am staying in Paris. I may or may not come to the country that weekend. What is sauce for the goose, I think.

I hunt through my closets for a short, tight jean skirt (I still have it somewhere) and a tight blouse and some high-heeled, cork-soled shoes. I brush my light shoulder-length hair out until it shines and dab perfume behind my ears.

I walk through the empty rooms that look onto formal

French gardens and stand at the window, waiting for him. Is this something I can really do? I have never made love to anyone but my unfaithful husband, after all.

Policemen in blue capes are closing the iron gates and blowing their whistles. A child cries, dragged reluctantly down a dusty path. A fan-shaped sprinkler catches the evening light in the spray.

He still has the dark, glossy hair and the broad shoulders. For a moment when he enters, in my panic I cannot remember his name. When he holds me to kiss me on the cheek, his eyes seem so close and such a deep blue, looking into them is like looking into a double-barrel gun. I say, "Michael! How amazing!" He, too, is called Michael! Of course—no wonder I have forgotten his name. He no longer sports the beard or the mustache and his lips look exposed, vulnerable.

He says, "Goodness, how extraordinary to see you again! How nice you look. You look terrific!" I grin. What he cannot see is the black lace bra and the thong I bought for the occasion, which rides up uncomfortably between my buttocks, as I sway a little and tell him I know a good place for dinner.

He apologizes for his informal attire. I look at the dusty South African shoes.

He is also married and has a small child, a little boy. I have not seen him, since I was sixteen. We go out for dinner somewhere simple in the neighborhood, and he tells me about his wife, his child, his work in the bush. He has come to Paris to find clients.

We drink red wine, and afterward I invite him back to the apartment I share with my husband. We walk through the streets of Paris, holding hands. We sit together on the elegant green leather couch before the French doors and he puts his arm around me. He says, "Don't worry, it will be quick," which it is.

The next morning he joins me, and we leave early to drive down to our old mill in the Loiret, where my husband and the children are waiting for us for lunch. After lunch my lover (*I have a lover! I have a lover!* I say to myself, ready to put an announcement in the papers) and I go out walking, and I show him the flat, wheat-growing fields of the Beauce, and he tells me about his life in the army in Rhodesia. He gets his socks wet, and I ask my husband to lend him a dry pair. He has to leave that evening, but before he goes, he looks at me with wonder and says, "I didn't know you were still in love with me."

"Neither did I," I respond quite truthfully.

After he has gone, my husband says casually, "Nice fellow but not too bright," words that probably ring the death knell on the affair.

Still, the lover sends me a large bouquet of red roses, with a note inviting me to come to Africa to visit him.

I actually do go to visit him. I fly to Salisbury and go out in the bush with him. I remember lying beside him on the yellow sand, my head propped on a deadwood branch under the fever trees beside the wide, dark, swift-moving water of the Limpopo. While he unbuttons my blouse, I watch the sudden flash of brilliance, as a kingfisher dives for its prey.

Later that night in the tent I hear a rustle and a scratching at the tent and the cry of a lion. He reassures me, "It's only an anteater. It's looking for eggs," he says, and then he throws my legs up over my head and makes love to me in a sort of shoulder stand! Is this what my mother-in-law had in mind? Certainly, the lovemaking, at the very least, lessens the pain that Michael's constant vacillation continues to bring me. The Big White Hunter gives me back a little of my lost confidence in myself. I can only hope my sister, too, has had some moments when she was able to enjoy the peace of a summer's night, the smells of the earth, the freedom and delight of her young body.

XXXVI

LAST GLIMPSES

MAXINE STAYS WITH US ONE LAST SUMMER IN THE HOUSE WE have built in Sardinia on the Costa Smeralda, where she manages to come with only one of her daughters.

I see her lying under the red-and-white-checked canopy of the guest bedroom with its view of the blue plumbago in the garden and beyond that, the scintillant Mediterranean Sea.

That is when she tells me that she is frightened to go back home. "But you have to go back to the other children," I will say, to my eternal regret. Her death remains unimaginable to me, though I fear it.

Then my sister comes back to Paris with me in late August to outfit Cybele for her departure at sixteen for the fancy boarding school in Connecticut, where she will be so unhappy. Together we carefully choose her clothes, as though they could protect her, shield her from the hurts we fear for her, despite our hopes. The three of us sit out in a café on Avenue Matignon, one sunny afternoon.

I have a handful of last memories of my sister: that moment in Paris, and the last one when I say good-bye to her in the street in Geneva.

In Paris I tell my sister how unhappy I am to think my darling deaf daughter will be so far away from me, how I will miss her at such a distance from home.

"How can anyone be unhappy in this beautiful place?" she says, sitting smiling in the sunshine, sipping a café au lait in an outdoor café under a red awning, looking along the wide boulevard with wonder, blinking the thick dark lashes of her big violet eyes, relishing the last of the Parisian summer, this last moment of peace and warm companionship.

I see her for the last time in Geneva. She is accompanied by her accountant, a stocky, dark-haired man, Sean, much older than her, who I imagine may also be her lover. I remember the respectful way he pulls back her armchair in a restaurant in the hotel where we are staying, the Hôtel du Rhône, where the white river rushes down its banks outside our window. I remember my sister arriving in the early morning to knock on the door of our hotel room, looking flushed and happy.

The accountant has come ostensibly to help my sister

retrieve her money. Her husband has moved it from a joint account and put it into his own name. Somehow the accountant, who had once been Carl's friend, has managed to acquire a power of attorney from him and now has access to the money.

I see him with the sun behind him, striding across a bridge in Geneva. He is carrying the gold bars in the fancy new briefcase my sister has given him, going across the bridge to put them in another bank, where they will be safe for her, or so we believe. In the end the children will never have access to this money, which the accountant keeps for himself.

My sister and I wander together around the old town of Geneva and sit out in a square and drink tea and talk about our childhood in the beautiful garden in Johannesburg. We talk about the games we played together, how we spread mulberries all over our faces, made garlands of flowers and wound them around our heads. We speak of our common ancestors, our grandfather who came out from a small town in southern Germany and started the timber firm where our father made his money.

We talk about money. "What would we do without any money?" she asks me. It is a fear that lingers. "Easy come, easy go," as my mother-in-law once snidely said to me, implying I was too casual with the money that had landed so easily in my lap. Yet the lack of any kind of permanence is what we rightly fear. Our lives are already marked by our losses: our father, who has left us when we were so young; our mother's frequent departures into a world of her own; the husbands we have chosen, and who have almost destroyed who we are.

Yet I expect to see my sister again soon. So close to death, she has plans to change her life, I know, to leave her husband and start out anew. Oddly, this will be what Ouma says to me at Maxine's funeral: "She had so many new, exciting plans." Poised on the brink of death, Maxine feels free, ready to live again. With her boundless curiosity, her sympathy for others, her intelligence, she loves the beauty of the world around her, the smells of summer, the light in the leaves of the trees, life.

I say good-bye in the street for what will be the last time. She stands in the sunshine, and the wind whips her blond curls across her high forehead, and the light sleeves of her cream sundress beat against her smooth young arms like little wings. She is thirty-nine years old when she is killed, leaving six children. Her youngest child is three years old.

XXXVII

INTERLUDE

I HAVE TRIED AGAIN AND AGAIN TO IMAGINE HER LAST MO-
ments, as though, if I could imagine them, put them into
words, they would not happen, as if I could arrest the passage of time, stop the film, rewind.

He leads her by the hand from the party where they have
spent their last evening, drinking, eating, and dancing.

She lingers on the dance floor, turning and twisting with
friends in the flashing lights, until her husband insists they
leave. They walk across the lawn to their car, the sky wild
with stars, all the sounds of the spring night coming to
them; the elegant blond surgeon, slim, accomplished, in his
white suit; his wife wearing a thin blue dress, the skirt a little tight at the waist. She has gained weight, and her unruly
curls fall over her face. Perhaps, too, she has drunk too much

wine. He is always filling her glass. She wears the pearl ring with the diamonds Mother has given her, which is how her eldest daughter will identify the shattered body with its broken wrists and ankles.

She stops a moment to fix the strap of her high-heeled sandal, where a stone has caught. She leans on him. Her friend and hostess is still standing at the door, watching them walk across the lawn, as she has watched them through the evening. "He seemed in a bad mood, glowering at her as she danced," she told me, "but, hey, he was often in a bad mood, wasn't he? I put it down to the kind of work he had to do."

My sister turns to say good-bye. "I thought she was having a really good time," her friend told me, sadly, years later, when I questioned her. "How she loved to dance, loved a party, music."

For a moment my sister seems to hesitate, standing in the ghostly light of the moon, as though she is considering going back to the party. But her husband says something that from that distance her hostess cannot hear. Perhaps he says, "Come on. I'm dead-tired. I have to get up early tomorrow morning to operate." So she just lifts her arm, waves good-bye, and they go on to where he has parked the silver convertible Mother had given them as a wedding present. It is the last time her friend sees her alive.

My sister gets into the car, and her husband sits beside

❦

her in the dark. He buckles his seat belt. He is always reminding her to do likewise, but perhaps she does not bother, this night. She glances at him. *We are not going far, after all,* she may have said, quite truthfully, and he would have nodded and watched, as she leaned back sleepily into the leather seat. His seat belt must be what saved him, only bruising his chest, one of the children will tell me later.

Perhaps, though, he may have been thinking of it for a long while. He would not have done it, if she had not said what she says in the car. He has been considering it for a while, or so his son tells me later. He found a gun at the back of his father's closet and was convinced at one point that his father was planning on killing the entire family. Later Vaughan will tell me instead that he thinks his father may have had a sort of minor stroke.

A friend of theirs, another doctor, has already done this, attempting to gas the whole family, but botching the job, some of the family living on, and some dying.

Probably she takes advantage of the fact that, for once, her husband has his hands safely on the wheel and his eyes on the road, to tell him what she has told me: that she is planning finally to leave him. Perhaps she has drunk enough at the party to give her the courage to tell him.

Despite all she has suffered at his hands I imagine she still expects him to behave the way she would behave. Perhaps that is what aggravates him so, her continuing hopefulness. Probably she believes they are near enough to the house by then, that she is safe.

It is a warm spring evening in October, and the top is down and the radio playing loudly. Perhaps she asks him to turn down the music, because it would disturb the sleeping children. Or she sucks on her teeth in the way that annoys him. Or perhaps he says something about the way she had been carrying on at the party, that she looked like a slut, dancing like that in her thin blue dress. He is always telling her that he has put her up on a pedestal, and she has fallen from it into the dirt. Perhaps she turns to him with rage and says she is going to leave him, that she despises him.

Or most probably she says nothing at all.

At the last minute, he apparently swerves slightly away from the lamppost. Perhaps had he swerved a little more they might both have lived. It must be harder to do than you would think—killing yourself, I mean.

XXXVIII

LINGERING ON

I LINGER ON IN SOUTH AFRICA AFTER MY SISTER'S FUNERAL, staying with my mother and my Aunt Pie. I sleep in my aunt's room, and she moves out onto the narrow covered veranda, as I recall. I remain for weeks, leaving my own children with Michael, taking my breakfast with Mother in her bedroom, where she sits up, eating her anchovy toast in her bed in her mauve nightgown, while I try to persuade her to prosecute my brother-in-law.

I feel I cannot go on with my life without some kind of closure to my sister's. She cannot rest in peace, until I have found some kind of solution to her unjust death. Why had I not kept her with me safely in Paris? Her death fills me with guilt, and all her past comes to me with arms outstretched, begging me to avenge her. I think of what Antigone says: "It

is the dead, not the living, who make the longest demands."
As each day passes, her memory is being slowly effaced,
rubbed out. She is slipping away in silence. I want to hold on
to her, to gather her up in my arms, hold her safe, protect
her, when it is too late. I will defy her enemies.

Why this search for revenge? Because I am her, and she
is me, and I keep turning back to that moment in the dark
when she put out her hands and feet to brace herself against
the dashboard, the moment when her heart was still beating
wildly, the southern stars still shining brilliantly above her,
and all the night flowing through her like a tide.

She stands there, the wind in her curls, and I kiss her
cheek. Like Orpheus I cannot stop looking back.

I lie on my aunt's bed and weep. When I finally fall asleep,
my aunt wakes me rudely, striding through the room, rum-
maging in a drawer. My aunt, who is so good with babies, has
little patience now with me.

My presence, my grief, above all my desire for vengeance
are all unwanted here, extraneous, disturbing. I am taking up
my aunt's space. I have turned her out of her room. She finds
my presence unsettling, unnecessary. My grief, I sense, she
considers histrionics, exaggerated, useless, and self-indulgent.

This is a world where appearances, above all, count, where
sorrow is not expressed. We are all pretending that all is for
the best in the best of worlds, even a tragedy of this kind.

We are expected to go on bravely without complaining or voicing what we feel in our hearts.

My aunt has other motives for wanting to separate me from my mother. She wants my mother's money for herself and her own daughter. She wants her peace of mind. She comes rushing into Mother's bedroom in the morning, her coffee cup trembling in hand, never leaving Mother on her own with me. Mother is her livelihood, her daughter's. Is she afraid Mother might give me the money? She wants to find out what is happening.

I look up at her now in her room, as she fumbles around in her dressing table for something.

I say, "I am the one who should have died." In a way I feel I have died. I am being carried forward like my sister on the river of death. She and I are one, have been commingled from the start. Who saw my dead father lying on his bed? Was it she or me? Who is now dead? Should it not be me?

"Don't talk such nonsense," my Aunt Pie says.

XXXIX

SEARCHING FOR HER SPIRIT

I VISIT MY SISTER'S HOUSE DAILY, THE BIG SPRAWLING HOUSE with the slippery corridors and the brick walls that she had built by a deaf architect, with the garden laid out by his sister, the fountain that runs over a brick wall into the pool, the sloping green lawns, the oak trees, the tennis court.

I walk into her big bedroom, her bathroom with its bright patio and bitter aloes. I open up her closets, lift a pink silk shirt to my nose, and root out her smell, her essence, trying to evoke her spirit. There in her rooms I feel her gentle presence hovering. I seem to see the shadow of her movements, and her protecting aura comes to me now, her tenderness. She enfolds me in her warm arms, as she did as a child.

Her sister-in-law and the sister-in-law's husband have already moved into the big house with their two small children.

It is Mother, I assume, who decides Carl's sister should care for Maxine's children, though I offer to take the four older ones to Paris with me, but this offer is turned down. This way the children can remain together in their own house, continue at their private schools in the familiar routine of their days.

The sister-in-law, who has so valiantly taken on the house and six children in addition to her own two little ones, gives away some of my sister's things. She stands on the red-brick patio and calls out to me, "Would you like this?"

I go over to see what she has in her hand. It is the pink enamel Hermès bracelet I remember my sister buying in Paris. I have a matching blue one. "The children?" I ask, holding it in my hand.

"They have all the jewelry," she says, and hands me also the identical silk gown and nightdress in white, which I had bought in pink in Rome, or is it vice versa? I see my sister sitting on the edge of the boat-shaped Bernini fountain with the garlanded Spanish Steps behind. I remember my words of advice.

The sister-in-law goes through my sister's things, giving them away to her friends and family.

I play tennis with the older children and hide-and-seek with the little ones in their garden. I tell stories. I am loath to leave them, to leave the place where my sister has lived and died.

XL

REVENGE

Above all, I am loath to leave Carl unpunished. I cannot but consider him my sister's murderer; I cannot bear to see him get off without any penalty at all, scot-free. My brother-in-law is hospitalized after my sister's death, apparently seriously wounded. He has, clearly, head injuries. There has been damage to the brain during the accident, we are told. His long-term memory does not seem to be affected. It is just the short-term that has gone. How useful is this to him?

How much damage has really been done is not clear. Is he simply lying low? He lies for weeks in the hospital, hardly speaking, recovering slowly, we are told.

My mother insists we go and visit. Reluctantly, I accompany her. I stand in silence by his bedside, hardly able to move,

❀

to look at him. My mother sits by his bed and holds his hand without apparent anger or blame.

Is it too painful for her to blame him? Yet, she was the one who said from the start that she knew he would kill Maxine. I remember how she would call me and say, "Black-and-blue! Black-and-blue! He beats her black-and-blue." Why had none of us done anything to stop this? Why had we not engaged a bodyguard to sit at the door? Each time he beat her, she would retire to my mother's cottage, but each time she would go back to her husband, eventually. He would apologize, promise, threaten with reprisals, the classic scenario with a South African twist.

Yet when I ask my mother to hire a lawyer, to go with me and make a declaration to the police, to have him punished for this crime, she simply says, "Think of the children. It is their father, all they have left. They have suffered enough. We must avoid a scandal at all costs for their sake."

No one speaks of what has really happened. As usual, the truth is muffled, covered up, silenced. No one in the family wants any trouble. Mother says, "He has been sufficiently punished. Besides, it would be impossible to convict him of murder." The car crash will be treated as an accident.

"We could get a good lawyer," I say, incensed. A lawyer cousin suggests I try to hire Sydney Kentridge, the lawyer who played a leading role in a number of political trials, who defended Mandela during the Treason Trial and Stephen Biko's family in 1978, proving indubitably that Biko went into the interrogation room alive and well and came out a physical wreck, dying subsequently alone, a miserable and terrible death in his prison cell.

Mother refuses.

She continues to go to the hospital and sit by my brother-in-law's bedside, and holds his hand with extraordinary and perhaps exemplary lack of anger or desire for revenge. My mother-in-law will say she is *un duro falso*, a false hard one.

I overhear my Aunt Pie say to my mother, referring to me, "I wish she would just go home. She's just stirring up trouble."

XLI

DESIRE

But I do not go home; I cannot. I am held here hostage in the grip of great grief and bent on seeking revenge. Like Antigone I want to honor the dead, avenge injustice. I seek some kind of closure. Surely my brother-in-law should be punished for what he has done. Why are we all paralyzed, passive?

I seek out anyone who can give me information, anyone who knew my sister well, as though they could bring her close to me, help me to avenge her. I want them to talk about my sister, to tell me what they know about her. I want to know all the secrets of her well-guarded heart.

I meet with one of my sister's financial advisers. We sit silently opposite one another in the dimly lit booth of a restaurant. There are artificial flowers behind the man's glossy head. He has dark blue eyes, luxuriant lashes, dark hair, well-manicured hands. An attractive man, I think incongruously for a moment with a flicker of desire, with his broad shoulders and blue eyes, the bright flash of a smile.

Somehow this death has left me open, exposed, desirous. I think of Tolstoy's mourners in *The Death of Ivan Ilych*, each one happy *he* has not died, each one thinking of how the death of his beloved friend can be used to advance his affairs.

Yet, what I want is to follow my sister into death. I would prefer to be the dead one or at least to know how this death came about.

The financial adviser says her affairs have been left in good order. Her husband and the children will inherit a considerable fortune.

"Carl will inherit some of her money?" I ask, appalled. He nods.

"Surely she never left him any money," I say.

I stare into his blue eyes. He says, "There's a will. He gets a seventh part. Don't worry, the six children have been left well endowed. The money will protect them. You should let your mother know."

When I do tell Mother, we are in the car with my Aunt Hazel, the youngest of the three sisters. Mother tells me for the first time that none of the grandchildren will get much when she dies. "When I have taken care of my own family," she says, looking at Hazel, who smiles smugly, "there will not be much left for anyone else," which will, indeed, be the case. The nine grandchildren will split between them only one million of the eight million rands she leaves, the other seven going to her family, this in the days when the rand was worth something.

I think of Mother saying to us as children, "Everything I have is yours." Is she now going to leave my father's money to others? Does she now hate me, because I am alive, and her firstborn is dead? Can she no longer bring herself to love a child of hers? Has her excessive love turned to hate? Yet she will do nothing to avenge her daughter's death. She seems frozen, filled with drugs and grief.

XLII

A PLAN

Sean is the only one to come up with a plan. He approaches me in the garden after the funeral, and for a moment I cannot think who he is. Then I remember our meeting in Switzerland, his hand hovering on the arm of my sister's chair, my sister's flushed cheeks, as she stands at dawn in the doorway of our hotel room. I think of the new shiny briefcase Maxine had bought him, with which he had transferred her gold bars to another numbered account. I wonder what has happened to the money.

He asks if we can meet. He has some photographs to show me.

I go to his house, a long, low white edifice very much like the other large houses on the street. There is a dog barking somewhere. He comes out of the front door, looking flustered, his tanned skin flushed. He greets me warmly on the steps and ushers me inside the low-ceilinged living room. There are toys on the carpet, and the venetian blinds are drawn on the light. He wants me to meet someone, he says.

There is another man there, a stranger, lurking in the shadows, a thin, pale, fair-haired man in a tweed jacket despite the warm air. He is smoking a cigarette and gets to his feet, when I enter the room, shakes my hand. He is introduced, though the name means nothing to me, and I wonder what he is doing here.

We all sit down and a plump older woman in an apron comes out with a tray with coffee and Marie biscuits. We exchange banalities. Sean suggests we go out into the back garden. There the three of us sit around a table, the two men facing me. Then Sean picks up the white envelope he brought out with him. He takes out his photographs to show me the road where my sister was killed.

"No skid marks, no other car in sight—you can see the road is dry. And whatever he is, he's not a drinker," the accountant says.

The other man says, "A surgeon. He's wearing his seat belt, and she is not. This was obviously a deliberately violent act."

I nod my head and wonder what he wants me to do.

"Perhaps an impulsive one. He was an impulsive man. He may have wanted to kill himself, too," I say.

"You must know there was a history of violence. He was always beating her up," the accountant says.

"I know, I know," I say, thinking of my sister lying in the canopied red bed, the windows open on the view of the sparkling blue Mediterranean. She is saying, "I don't want to go home. I'm afraid." It is the last time she came to Sardinia, and then went on with us to Paris. Why did I tell her to go back to her children? What good is she to them now?

I ask what we can do and explain that my mother is against any sort of trial or public action. "She's worried about the scandal, the effect on the children, understandably," I explain and add that it might be difficult to prove his guilt in a court of law. "To be fair, this was probably a botched murder-suicide, and he's all that is left to these poor children."

"Not much good to anyone as far as I'm concerned," he mutters.

"Still their father, for better or for worse," I say.

The other man in the small fenced garden leans forward at this point and stubs out his cigarette. He tells me that he knows one way to handle a situation of this kind. I look from him to Sean inquiringly. He now explains this man is a private detective. He has taken the liberty of inviting him here today, as he is used to handling matters of this kind. I stare at the stranger. "How? How could we handle this?" I ask.

The detective looks at me and says that in his opinion

the best way, perhaps the only way, to handle this situation at this point, would be to get rid of the husband. For a certain price my brother-in-law could be quite easily removed.

I have the feeling none of this is real. I have entered some kind of crime story or a film. I look at the house, the shuttered windows. I imagine this man's office, his name on the pebbled glass door. I imagine someone slipping into the hospital in the night, going along the corridor with something in his hands: an ax, a noose, a knife?

The detective lights up another cigarette and says he knows someone who could handle this quickly and easily for a certain price. For a moment I actually consider the offer, seeing it in my mind's eye like a word deleted on a page.

Finally, of course, I say that we were not brought up in that way, that I could not live with something like that, my sister would never have wanted me to do something of that kind.

Would she? I wonder.

XLIII

ARMS

My brother-in-law, once he leaves the hospital, will live with his family until he starts to hit his sister, or so Mother will tell me. He is then obliged to leave the house but eventually remarries a colleague, a plastic surgeon, who, I am told, was always in love with him, though now that they are married, she locks him up in the house and will not allow him out. It is she who bullies him. Life has a way of evening out the injustices it has created.

They will move to the Eastern Cape to a town called Hogsback. He will continue in the operating room, though, in a neat reversal worthy of fiction, only passing the instruments to his surgeon-wife.

His children will occasionally visit him. They take care

of him. Perhaps they even love him. He will never be accused of murder or anything else, for that matter. The children do what is necessary for them to go on bravely with their lives. He remains for all of them, of course, their father, whatever he may or may not have done.

Years later, Carl attends the wedding of his eldest boy, sitting, smiling, at the bridal table. I, too, am invited and am asked to read something during the church service. I choose a passage from Spenser's *Prothalamion*:

> *And make your joys redound*
> *Upon your bridal day, which is not long:*
> *Sweet Thames, run softly, till I end my song.*

I manage to get through the ceremony and reception without shaking Carl's hand.

The only weapon left to me is to write about what has happened in fictional form. None of the family want this story told, neither his family, naturally, nor even my own. No one wants to tell the children what must have happened, though surely they, or at least the older ones, must know better than anyone else. All of them will tell me of scenes of terrible violence, of beatings to the point of unconsciousness, glasses being thrown across the room, scars left on the face. And there is now my brother-in-law himself to contend with, alive and relatively well, living in the Cape.

I have been writing in my head, telling stories to children, writing diaries, reading and remembering, all my life, but it is not before the death of my sister that I actually sit down and write a complete novel. I am determined to keep her alive on the page. Here, I can give her the revenge she would have wanted to have. I can control her destiny.

Once I am back in Paris, I sit at my glass-topped desk in the living room in the apartment on the Rue Guynemer with the chestnut trees outside and the ghostly dome of the Panthéon visible in the mist through the leaves. I write about my sister's life and death. After her sudden and tragic death I pour out a novel in three months and send it off to a publisher.

I write in a rage. I want to expose the murderer, weep for the murdered one, blame the guilty. I want to write as a witness to a crime. I want to say, *Look at the injustice! Look at this wicked man! Look! Look at what he did to my sister!* I want to say like Jane Eyre, *Unfair! Unfair!*

Initially, I do not think of the danger or inconvenience to anyone of putting this all down on the page.

The novel, in any case, is promptly turned down. I have

the gall to call the editor up and ask why my book has been rejected. She is kind enough to take my call and answer me. She says quite simply, "It was not good enough." She asks me how it could have been good enough. "How long did it take you to write this?" she asks. "How long have you been writing?" she wants to know.

XLIV

DEPARTURE

ONE EVENING, NOT LONG AFTER MY SISTER'S DEATH, MICHAEL comes in late again. I'm lying on the green and gold bedspread on our double bed in the bedroom, which has the stained-glass windows looking onto the inner courtyard, as if it were a church. It has once been the dining room in the apartment on the Rue Guynemer.

I am reading (this is true, I promise you) Dickens's *Hard Times*. I look up from the pages and say, without thinking, "If you are going to fuck your mistress, why don't you just stay with her for dinner as well?"

"How did you know?" he asks, his face crumpling up like a child's, as he drops down beside me on the bed, holding his head in his hands.

"I didn't know," I say quite truthfully, looking at him, hardly able to breathe.

This one he tells me is called Leopoldine! It even rhymes with the first one's name! She has short dark hair, I believe, but this time I do not ask for any details. I do not want to hear about any adorable scar on a lip or Leopoldine's guilt or even her cancer of the uterus. This one is too much even for me. Surely lightning does not strike the same tree twice. This time I just tell him not to bring his laundry home anymore, please!

When my two older girls, Sasha and Cybele, have both left for college in America, and my youngest is admitted to the French Lycée in New York, I finally decide to leave and go back to school myself. I will go to Columbia and do an MFA in writing. I will acquire the necessary skills to write the story I have to write. I will learn how to spin this tale, so that someone else will be caught up in its web.

Sasha will be nearby at Barnard, and Cybele in New Haven at Yale, where her father studied, and where she will be the first deaf student to graduate.

I finally decide to leave Michael, leave the beautiful apartment on the Rue Guynemer, the house in Pithiviers, the villa in Sardinia and go back to New York with Brett and study the art of writing. Has it taken my sister's death to allow me to move forward in this way?

I find a small furnished apartment in a large ugly modern

building in the Seventies that looks over the Hudson. Like my mother with Crossways at the death of my father, I leave all the furniture, the china, the silver, the piano, everything behind. At the time none of this means much to me. I want to write my sister's story. I want the truth to be known. I want to follow her on the page.

XLV

MOTHER TONGUE

AT COLUMBIA IT IS FALL, AND I SIT LOOKING THROUGH THE
windows at the leaves of the chestnut trees, swaying in the soft
air, listening to the cadences of my own language with joy. I
have been in France for fourteen years, have done all my long
studies: history of art at the École du Louvre, psychology at the
Institut Catholique, French civilization at the Sorbonne, several degrees in the French language. I have read the great
French authors—Corneille, Racine, Molière, Flaubert, Proust,
Sartre, Camus—in French. I have read Marguerite Duras and
marveled.

But now I am ecstatic to be surrounded again by people
who speak my mother tongue. I am overjoyed to hear it spo-
ken by my professors, particularly the poets, like Richard

Howard, who stands before us in class, so dramatically, in his cape and monocle, using words I have to look up afterward in the dictionary. I feel my way back into my own language *à tâtons*, haltingly. Words come to me in French, when I am speaking English. I am confused, searching for the right word.

Have I forgotten how to speak my own language? Have I lost myself in these foreign languages, rather than finding out who I am?

I must now take the plunge back into the pool, back into the clear calm waters from whence I came. I am returning to my origins, to English, the language with the most words in the world, the language of Shakespeare, the language of the King James Bible, my mother tongue.

I had left this language to find myself as an adolescent, to establish my independence, to take on a disguise that would enable me to be who I really was. Yet it is coming back to English, I now realize, back to the writers who have nourished my early dreams and desires, who have created the characters—Becky Sharp and Amelia from *Vanity Fair*, Cathy from *Wuthering Heights*, Jane Eyre, Dora and Agnes from *David Copperfield*—heroines I have emulated, tried to copy, who have become part of me. It is by writing in this language, my first language, my mother tongue, that I realize I will find myself and perhaps the answers to the questions that trouble me.

It is in English that I will be able to tell the true story of my sister's life and death. It is in coming back to what I know, recovering what I have lost, that I will have a second chance at life and at love.

XLVI

LOVE

In my early forties I am older than most of the other students in my classes at Columbia, but I notice one woman with gray in her short hair, who wears thick glasses. Despite her smooth skin and youthful appearance I imagine she must be even older than I am.

She is also, I discover, an excellent writer, one of the few students who has published work. She reads my work and comments generously, and I read hers with awe.

I tell her something of my story, and she asks me one day if I would like to meet someone new, someone who was once a student of her husband's, a psychiatrist. The man in question is a fine man from a fine family and remarkably well educated, she says. He has studied at all the best schools, Harvard and Yale, and has done his medical degree at Columbia.

Knowing I am an Anglican, she asks me if I mind that the man is Jewish.

"On the contrary," I say, thinking perhaps of my mother's elopement with her first husband to Kimberley in her youth.

"He's a good man, do you know what I mean?" she asks me.

I say yes, but I'm not sure I do at all, though I will find out.

We meet one evening in a Japanese restaurant in Greenwich Village. I see the man approach, coming out of the evening shadows, walking fast, with small steps, already waving his fine hands. He has a shock of white hair, large, close-set dark eyes, an aquiline nose, a sweet voice. He comes from the Midwest and sounds to me like a cowboy.

We sit opposite one another, and my friend and her husband sit beside us. The man, Bill, has two little boys, eight and eleven. We all talk about our children, an apparently safe subject. As we talk, I am afraid I might make a grammatical error with this hyper-educated man, and I am certain he must be counting my wrinkles.

We are, it turns out, the same age: forty-two—so old, I think at the time. Why is it that when one is young, one feels old, and when one is old, one feels young?

At the end of the meal, Bill, the psychiatrist, who sits opposite me, turns slightly green and asks me, "Would you like to have a coffee with me?"

I stare back at him. There is a hushed and expectant silence at the table, all eyes on me.

"But how will I get home?" I ask, as though New York City has suddenly been transformed into the wild African veld of my childhood.

"I could, perhaps, drive you there?" he says softly, his voice rising slightly at the end of the sentence.

We do have coffee and then some. He takes me to a famous coffee shop called Le Figaro, and we talk. He seems so interested in what I have to say. "I have never heard anyone say something like that before," the clever man says in response to some banal remark I make. I think, *What a long time since I have had such an interesting conversation with such an intelligent man.*

We go back to his apartment on Washington Street, and he shows me his domain. It is a curiously open space, rather like its owner, I will discover. It is made up of five open floors, like layers of a mille-feuille cake: his office with its separate entrance lies beneath the living room, above which is a sleeping loft with his boys' beds, then a dining room and kitchen, and at the top, a bedroom with the TV on the floor and a half-moon window. There are the two entrances and one red-brick wall that connects it all. From the top floor one can hear the murmur of voices down at the lowest level.

We sit on his cream sofa in the living room, and eventually, when I suggest it might be more comfortable to do what we are doing in a bed, he takes me up the stairs to his bedroom with the half-moon window and the white statues of Schiller and Goethe, who look down on us solemnly in their long frock coats, as we lie on the bed on the floor. Somewhere in the room I hear a hamster, who runs in his little cage, going around and around.

Somehow—how do these things happen?—I fall in love with this man, or perhaps into passion would be a better way of putting it. Perhaps it has something to do with his background, his education, his fine mind.

I see him, too, eventually, with his two little boys, whom we take skiing with us one weekend. I notice with a pang of longing the way he puts his hand so gently, so lovingly, on their dark heads.

I meet his father in St. Louis, a tall, distinguished man who comes out to show me his first editions. He brings me his beautiful books like a gift, like a child showing off what he has that is most precious.

I meet his mother, an energetic lady who has become a professor of photography and organizes photography shows. They are both great lovers and patrons of the arts, the kind of parents I sometimes think I would have liked to have.

Perhaps, too, after a year on my own in New York, I am

starved for affection, love, or is it just sex? Perhaps I just like this man's smell, his smooth skin, his slim firm body, his voice. Like the elements in a good story there is no way to define love.

Though we are so different in so many ways, we seem also to be kindred souls, with our Germanic background (his grandfather has come from Berlin, as mine has from Kempten in Bavaria), our diligence, and our ability to work hard, to bear down and concentrate for long hours. We both believe we are here to perform some useful function, to give back to the community whatever our particular gifts might provide. Neither of us can remain idle for very long. We are both stubborn, determined, and ready for a fight.

Whatever it is, I come rushing to him whenever he summons me, arriving too early at night, when his patients have not yet left, obliged to wander around the block in the snow with a basket of food for him like Little Red Riding Hood: soups, stews, and compotes, the food from my colonial childhood, which he later confesses he does not enjoy.

I wait for him to call in a state of anxiety that borders on panic. I hear the telephone ring in my dreams. I do not believe easily in permanence of any kind, and he makes no long-term promises. We see one another once or sometimes twice a week. My panic gradually becomes almost unbearable. At one point I come close to suggesting that I move in with him, but he says, "For that to happen, there would have to be love." At which point I get up and leave his apartment in a rage.

Finally I have the courage to tell him that I would prefer to call him rather than waiting for his calls. And eventually, despite the English food or whatever reluctance he may have had to overcome he consents to have me move into his apartment in the Village.

XLVII

MOTHER

One night in March, soon after I have met Bill, I receive a call. It is my Aunt Hazel, who tells me that my mother has died.

I fly out to South Africa for the funeral with Cybele, who is twenty years old, now a junior at Yale. I am not sure why she is the only one of my girls who comes with me, but I do know she loved her grandmother very much, and her grandmother loved her.

Mother's great gift was her capacity to love without conditions, without reason or return. She reached out to those who needed her love and care the most. She was drawn to my deaf daughter instinctively, I felt. Often she would just reach out and grasp her hand and say, "Are you happy, my dear?" whereas my mother-in-law would say, "When you have guests over, Sheila, you shouldn't feel obliged to bring Cybele into the living room, you know, my dear." My mother accepted Cybele as she was, loved her for who she was: a wild child with her tantrums and anger and the frustration of her incomprehension. She reached out to her and ultimately left her more money than she did my other girls, because she felt it would be harder for her to make a living.

Though I must have been told about this scene and never witnessed it, it remains one of my most distinct memories: my mother and my Aunt Pie, carrying Cybele, who had thrown herself down on the sidewalk in a tantrum along a busy New York street. My aunt carries the feet and my mother, the hands, and they struggle along the pavement together. I imagine these two dignified middle-aged ladies in their corsets and flowered hats and gloves, carrying the screaming child through a bustling street of New York.

"What else could we do?" my mother said.

On the airplane Cybele and I sit together holding hands, remembering. This time I do not go to the morgue. I do not even want to see my mother lying in her coffin. She has been dead to me for a while. But Cybele goes and says she does not look like her grandmother: they have made her up, disguised her. She looks like someone else.

The last time I saw Mother was the Christmas before, when I went out to South Africa with Brett to visit her. She already appeared that way to me, dressed up and disguised, as if, as I had believed as a child, the witch had carried her away, taken her place.

She sat there so stiffly in her priceless jewels, her makeup and fine designer dress, unable to move or talk, in rigid silence, surrounded by her family, my aunts, my cousin, all her relatives, who hovered around her dutifully. Mother was filled with pills, alcohol, whatever she took, and surely, above all, great grief. At the time I felt she had drawn away from me completely. She was at a great distance. I had lost her long ago.

The loss of her older child and in such terrible circumstances must have killed something deep within her. She had little interest in her only remaining daughter, I sensed. Perhaps my presence was even painful to her. When I called and offered to come at Easter, she said, "Don't come, I don't want you to come." Perhaps, after losing one of her children, she could no longer reach out to the one who was left. Strangely, she turned back to her original family, her sisters, her brother, their children, all of whom closed the wagons around her, shut me out, no doubt knowing the end was near, and waiting impatiently for the will to bear its fruit. No one had told me she was dying, that I should rush to her side.

By the time I get out there for the funeral, one of the nephews has already taken off on an around-the-world trip. When the will is read I discover that Mother has not left any of my father's huge fortune to me. It all goes to her original family: her sisters, her brother, his wife, and all their numerous progeny, and also perhaps the love child of her youth. Who can blame these people for taking what she has so generously bestowed on them, and what they have worked so hard to acquire?

I realize then that despite my adolescent desire to escape my mother, to find myself in other languages, I will have ultimately to return to her, to my mother, my first sweetheart, to the beginning and the end. I will have to continue to write about her in my mother tongue.

I become aware in the writing that all the questions in my mind, all Mother's secrets, her early elopement at seventeen to Kimberley, her life with my father and his first wife at Crossways, even her increasingly excessive drinking and taking of drugs, all these are matters that are intimately entwined with my own and my sister's life and death. They are part of our childhood, part of our early and formative experiences, part of our upbringing. They are perhaps the basis of our vulnerability, our incapacity to protect ourselves, and also our capacity to reach out to others, albeit foolishly at times, to love.

In the end these silences and secrets will be Mother's great gift to me. They will propel me to the page in a quest to find the answers that lie behind these mysteries.

My mother and father.

The image she will leave with me is ultimately a joyful one. I see her in the sunlight on the glassed-in veranda at Crossways, twirling in her tight-fitting mauve dress, her slim ankles flashing, her legs twisting fast, and her tiny feet in her dainty high-heeled shoes, kicked high in the air, her dark curls clinging to her damp forehead. She is doing the Charleston, the windows open on the garden behind her, all the bright flowers, the nasturtiums, the orange cannas, the sweet peas in bloom; I see her filled with energy, enthusiasm, love for life.

XLVIII

WRITING IT DOWN

REPEATEDLY THEY COME TO ME ON THE PAGE: MY GHOSTS, MY mother with her arm thrown over her face in the green gloom of her high-ceilinged bedroom, my sister on the lawn in the sunlight, laughing, flowers in her curls. Others are there, too, absent friends, Enrico, standing in Mother's garden, watering the plants, my ex-husband, grinning his big baby grin, all those who have been with me in my youth.

But it is my dead sister who comes to me again and again. I bring her to life on the page, where I can keep her with me, close beside me, safe. I love describing her in a white dress, in blue, with her violet eyes, her soft smile, her gentle glance, her voice, her laugh.

In my first book, *The Perfect Place*, she is Daisy Summers,

Maxine as a little girl with flowers.

pretty, good, generous, and loving, the girl who lives with her three maiden aunts in a house on a cliff by the sea, the girl who will save a spider, catching it on the edge of a page, the girl whom the narrator denies she ever knew, the girl she is trying to forget. The narrator, the one who has survived to tell the tale, is the guilty one, the one who cannot feel, the friend who betrays her, who does not hear her cry for help, for love. The unnamed narrator looks elsewhere. She has her eye fixed on extraneous things: the landscape, a boat in the distance, a fork-tailed bird.

When the novel comes out in 1989, it will enjoy a certain literary success and will be published in several languages. A reader, himself a distinguished writer, will write and tell me that what he liked in the book was the "not knowing." My narrator will never be quite sure what has happened to Daisy Summers, just as it will never be proved what actually happened to my sister in the dark car that night. So many versions of the truth are possible, which enable me to tell the same story in so many different ways.

In story after story I conjure up my sister in various disguises, as well as other figures from our past. Her bright image leads me onward like a candle in the night. Again and again in various forms and shapes I write her story, colored by my own feelings of love and guilt. In *Cracks* she is Fiamma, the one who comes from afar, the beautiful foreigner

———————————— ❧ ————————————

with her Botticelli face, who understands all, who is the swimming coach, Miss G's, "Pet." She is surrounded by a group of swimmers, among them a certain Sheila Kohler, who will write it all down and will be part of the group who is responsible for her death.

I will combine here, in Miss G, echoes of Madame C, telling us, "No inhibitions here," and a writing teacher who would ask us, as Miss G does the girls, what is important in life: desire.

Gradually, over the years, I will learn to find a middle distance from the red-hot material of my sister's death.

I come closest to the actual events in a novel called *Crossways*. The book is told from three points of view: the woman who has lost a sister, the murderer himself, and a Zulu servant called John. At the end of the book it is the sister who remains, who returns to the house where she was born, who runs over the brother-in-law who has killed her sister in a car. Revenge and reversal are sweet, as they say—on the page, at least, if not in life.

Even in the historical novels I write, my sister appears in various forms. She is Emily Brontë, who dies so young, and she is the youngest of the three girls, too: Anne, who would so much have liked to live. She comes to me through the voice of those who have not been able to tell their story, like

Freud's young patient in *Dreaming for Freud*, who never gets to write down her version of what has happened, as my sister never will. To the voiceless, the muffled, the frightened, the guilty, I attempt to give words.

The danger of writing down the truth of my desires does not deter me, though it will cause me some grief, as the expression of truth often does. Naturally, my brother-in-law's family will be incensed, and his youngest sister will refuse to speak to me. This does not stop me. On the contrary, perhaps it will continue to propel me to the page in an effort to exorcise the demons, to allow my sister to speak through me.

I will actually write a novella, parts of which are published as "Correspondence" and "Invitation to a Voyage," about a woman living in France who writes a letter to her brother-in-law, asking him to come and do to her what he has already done to her sister. In the first page I write: "I presume it was not difficult for you. It probably came upon you of a sudden, as they say. Perhaps there was a moment of exhilaration, something approaching ecstacy, a moment when you felt more alive than you had ever done before." Was this how Carl felt, driving in the dark?

Later, too, I will write about the brother-in-law who comes after the remaining sister, who knows what he has done to her sister. He comes to New York and follows her in a dark street.

———————————— ❧ ————————————

My mind turns back obsessively, as it does so often with trauma, returning to this theme in various permutations in an attempt to find meaning in the absurdity of our lives.

I do not know if my brother-in-law ever reads these books or stories, but, curiously, one of my sister's children will tell me he has a novel by my eldest daughter, Sasha, by his bedside. My darling Sasha, too, has become a novelist, writing beautiful prose. I have told her that I know I am her material, as my own mother was mine, and she must use me as she thinks fit, which she does! In her first novel, *Angels in the Morning*, I am thinly disguised as a musician beating on the keys, while the children tumble down the bank and fall in the river! It is this book that my brother-in-law has by his bedside.

When Carl dies eventually, I have a sense of great relief but also of loss: this last conduit which has led me incessantly to my sister is now gone.

I publish thirteen books with various publishing houses, and dozens of short stories and essays in a variety of magazines. Writing becomes my pleasure, my passion, my obsession, my constant compulsion, stemming from a deep need to share my story with others, a way of establishing a community of souls, of reaching out to my fellow man, and a means of both escaping and exploring my own mind and heart. It is an attempt to answer the questions that continue to perplex and

Standing together on the bridge over the fishpond
with bows in our hair.

trouble me. Above all, perhaps, it is a way to hold those I have loved and lost in my mind and in my heart of hearts.

My sister has been dead now for more than thirty-five years, but I still see her in the garden at Crossways. We are down in the bamboo, hiding in the thick stalks, playing Doll. I hear the rustle of the leaves in the wind.

Maxine lies stiffly before me, doll-like, blinking her violet eyes at me, her cheeks flushed in the heat, tilting her head up toward me obediently, as she will in the end, showing me what I cannot believe, what I have had to come to see with my own eyes, that she, so lively and lovely, could be dead.

ACKNOWLEDGMENTS

OVER THE YEARS IN FICTION AND NONFICTION I HAVE WRITten about my life and, above all, about my sister's death. This memoir is peppered with sentences and subjects from previous works, though here in a very different form. I would like to thank the many editors from magazines, publishing houses, and anthologies who have so generously published my work:

Elizabeth Benedict, editor of *What My Mother Gave Me*
Sudip Bose at *The American Scholar*
Robert Boyers at *Salmagundi Magazine*
Richard Burgin at *Boulevard*
Ann Burt, editor of *My Father Married Your Mother*
Robert Fogarty at *The Antioch Review*
Daniel Jones at *The New York Times*
Elizabeth Gaffney at *The Paris Review*

Suzanne Kamata, editor of *Love You to Pieces*

David Leavitt at *Subtropics*

Gordon Lish at *The Quarterly* and at Knopf

Sandy McClatchy at *The Yale Review*

Cathy Medwick at *O, The Oprah Magazine* and *More*

Mark Mirsky at *Fiction*

Pat Towers at *O, The Oprah Magazine*

Roland Pease at *Zoland*

Bill Pierce and Sven Birkerts at *AGNI*

Dawn Raffel at *Redbook*

Andrea Richesin, editor of *Crush*

Raymond Smith and Joyce Carol Oates at *Ontario Review* and the Ontario Review Press

Rona Wineberg at *Bellevue Literary Review*

Particular thanks go to my agent, Robin Straus, and to Kathryn Court at Penguin for her faith, support, and wisdom, and to Sarah Stein.